NOTES ON THE HEBREW TEXT OF ISAIAH
Chapters XXVIII—XXXII

NOTES ON THE HEBREW TEXT OF ISAIAH

Chapters XXVIII—XXXII

BY

NORMAN H. SNAITH, M.A.

Tutor in Old Testament Languages and Literature,
Wesley College, Headingley, Leeds

THE EPWORTH PRESS

(EDGAR C. BARTON)

25-35 City Road, London, E.C.1

Made in *Great Britain*

PREFACE

THERE is no critical commentary in English on these particular chapters of the Book of the Prophet Isaiah, the nearest approach amongst modern books being G. H. Box, *The Book of Isaiah* (London, 1908), and the recent commentary under the same title by E. J. Kissane (2 vols., Dublin, 1941). These notes are an attempt to meet the need which arises from the fact that these chapters form the set portion in part of the London B.D. syllabus for 1946.

These notes are by no means to be regarded as taking the place of the many excellent exegetical commentaries which are in existence in English— namely, those by Cheyne, George Adam Smith (*Expositor's Bible*), Whitehouse (*Century Bible*), and especially Skinner (*Cambridge Bible*). This latter in two volumes we regard as being one of the most helpful and satisfactory commentaries ever written. In addition, there are the German critical and exegetical commentaries by Duhm, Marti and Procksch, in addition to the notes in Kittel's editions of the text, the notes being by Rudolf Kittel himself.

Every care has been taken to ensure accuracy, and no fantastic or even experimental suggestions have been included.

N. H. S.

ABBREVIATIONS

Aq,	Aquila.
LXX,	Septuagint.
MT,	Masoretic (Hebrew) Text.
OL,	Old Latin.
S,	Syriac (Peshitta).
Sym.,	Symmachus.
T,	Targum.
Th,	Theodotion.
V,	Vulgate.

BDB,	Oxford Lexicon.
DG,	Davidson, *Hebrew Grammar* (20th ed. onwards).
DS,	Davidson, *Hebrew Syntax*.
DT,	Driver, *Hebrew Tenses*.
EB,	*Encyclopædia Biblica*.
GK,	Gesenius-Kautzsch, *Hebrew Grammar*.
HDB,	*Hastings' Bible Dictionary*.
WL,	Wood and Lanchester, *Hebrew Grammar*.

The references are to pages, except in the case of
Gesenius-Kautzsch.

CHAPTER XXVIII

Verse 1. עֲטֶרֶת, cstr. s. of עֲטָרָה, fem. subst. meaning 'crown, wreath'. This abnormal cstr. form is sometimes found (GK 95*g*), and always (18 times) in connection with this substantive.

גֵּאוּת (majesty), not necessarily 'pride' in a bad sense, which properly is גַּאֲוָה. Presumably cstr. sing., though the Versions do not regard it as such. Translate 'Woe to the majestic crown of the drunkards of Ephraim', i.e. the city of Samaria.

שִׁכֹּרֵי, cstr. p. of שִׁכֹּר (drunkard). For the form, see GK 84ᵃ*e*, and for the construction, see GK 128*x*. LXX has μισθωτοί (hirelings), as if from the root שׂכר.

אפרים was formerly regarded as a true dual, but is now explained as an expansion from an original termination in -*an*, GK 88*c*.

צִיץ נבל וגֹ', usually translated 'and the fading flower of his glorious beauty', but this makes צִיץ a construct before the rest of the phrase with its qualifying adjective inserted immediately following it. This is most irregular, and is therefore explained as being 'used nominally and brought within the chain of constructs', DS 37. The cases here cited are doubtful, and the explanation in GK 128*w* does not meet the real difficulty. Vulgate and Douai have 'the glory of his joy' in apposition, which is better. Kissane suggests: 'and faded (see LXX) flowers is his splendid ornament'. Procksch omits the *vav* at the beginning, but it is better to regard it as introducing a causal

7

clause, cf. the instances given in GK 158a, and translate, 'for his glorious beauty is a fading flower', which both makes good sense, and also is sound syntax.

אֲשֶׁר. Not in LXX. Duhm and Cheyne omit here and also in verse 4 on the ground that the word is a frequent insertion of editors. On the other hand, Kittel would omit גֵּיא־שְׁמָנִים (fertile valley) as due to verse 4. Most commentators follow MT throughout, but the abs. for the cstr. is very difficult, and, according to GK 128c, is corrupt. It is better to follow Kittel, since LXX is not an accurate enough rendering of MT in either verse to justify any dogmatic statement as to what was read.

שְׁמָנִים, plural of intensity, DS 19 (Rem. 2), GK 124e.

הֲלוּמֵי, m. pl. cstr. of pass. ptc. qal of הלם (smite, as with a hammer), GK 128x. Cf. Proverbs xxiii. 35. LXX has 'drunken without wine', probably due to a reminiscence of xxix. 9. Kissane transfers the phrase to the end of 1a, retaining the rest of 1b.

Verse 2. חֹזֶק indeterminate. According to Skinner, the vagueness is in the prophet's mind and is an indication of an early date. Against this, the Assyrian menace must have been plain enough well before Tiglath-pileser made his expedition to the Mediterranean in 738 B.C., and probably as early as his accession in 745 B.C. It is better, therefore, to regard the construction as being analogous to the Arabic 'indeterminateness for the sake of amplication', GK 125c.

לַאדֹנָי. This is undoubtedly the true Masoretic reading. Cheyne and Box are wrong in following the לַיהוה of the two Soncino editions, which often do not agree with the Masora, particularly in respect of the Sacred Name. It is one of the 134 cases according to

8

the Masora where אדני is found for the Sacred Name. Vulgate and Douai omit the preposition, and so make the Lord Himself the mighty and strong one. Retain MT.

זרם is a downpour as of the cloud-masses of the monsoon rain, Psalm lxxviii. 18. Cf. Assyrian *zamaru* (to overwhelm).

שׂער (tempest), usually with *samech*, and only here with *sin*.

קמֶב, *qamets* with *athnach* in pause, the *a* being the primary sound, DG 40, WL 117 §3 (1), GK 29*k*, though see GK 93*q* with its reference to Hosea xiii. 14.

כבירים, 'like mighty waters overflowing'. Cf. the Spanish river Quadalquiver, which is the Arabic (Moorish) *Wad' el-Kebir*, 'the great river valley'.

הניח, 3 m. s. pf. of 2nd hiphil of נוח. Prophetic perfect, or perfect of certainty, DS 61, DT 17-21, GK 106*n*. 'He will lay down (i.e. as corn is laid by a rain-storm) to the ground with violence (RVm)', lit. 'with a hand', the article being omitted as at the beginning of the verse. Skinner takes the downpour of waters as the subject, and therefore treats the perfect as perfect of experience, DS 60, DT 17, GK 106*k*, translating by the English present. In this case the prep. *kaph* is the particle of comparison and a relative is understood, GK 155*g*. There are two hiphil forms of the verb נוח, the normal pf. הֵנִיחַ (impf. יָנִיחַ) with the true hiphil meaning 'cause to rest', and a second form, as here, with pf. הִנִּיחַ and impf. יַנִּיחַ, meaning 'deposit, place, leave, let remain', used mostly when the object either is, or is thought of as, inanimate. S read the impt. and connected the phrase with the following verse.

Verse 3. תרדמסנה עטרת, pl. verb and sing. subject. It would be correct to read either תֵּרָמֵס עֲטֶרֶת (so V) or תֵּרָמַסְנָה עֲטָרֹת. It is better to retain MT in spite of the syntactical difficulty, and to explain the anomaly by imagining the author to have been thinking here, as in verse 1, both of Samaria as the crown of the fertile valley, and of the festal crowns of the drunkards of Ephraim.

Verse 4. וְהָיְתָה. Most modern commentators would transfer this to the beginning of verse 4*b*, thus making it introduce the new simile of the early fig. In this case וציצת is read at the beginning of the verse, and a double subject is found for the plural verb in verse 3. So Cheyne, Duhm, Procksch, Kittel and others. It is better to retain MT, which is supported by the Versions, and to translate: 'And "the fading flower, his splendid ornament, which is at the head of the fertile valley" (thus quoting verse 1) shall be like the early fig before the autumn. . . .' Cheyne wishes to remove what he describes as 'the startling comparison of a flower to a fig', but he is in error here. The flower is not compared to the fig. The simile concerns the speed with which the flower fades and the speed with which the early fig is eaten by the finder, it being a delicacy much esteemed because of its size and sweetness.

ציצת. Apparently cstr. s. of ציצה, a feminine by-form of ציץ, not found elsewhere in OT and rare in Rabbinic writings. Read ציץ with Marti as in verse 1.

כבכורה, prep. *kaph* plus בִּכּוּרָה, possibly a shortened form of בִּכּוּרָתָה, which is בִּכּוּרָה plus 3 f. s. suffix. All the examples of this (four in all) are uncertain, and they should be emended by omitting the *mappiq*, so

GK 91*e*, and most moderns. The reference is to the 'early fig' of late June, much larger and sweeter than the normal fig which ripens in October. קיץ means 'autumn' and not 'summer', so that all three words together describe the early fig, 'the first ripe fig before the autumn'.

אשר is a relative and not a pronoun, here meaning 'which when'. Even when it appears to be equivalent to the English 'who', the pronominal subject should be regarded as being included in the verb rather than in the relative.

יראה, impf. of 'general custom', GK 107*g*, DG 157 par. I 2 (1), DS 65*f*, DT 38. The construction is that of the indefinite personal subject; cf. the French *on*, the German *man*, and the use of 'the man' in 1 Samuel ix. 9. It is exactly comparable to the Arabic use of the indeterminate participle, GK 144*e*, DS 109 (top). Translate 'which when any one sees, he swallows it up . . .'

בעודה, prep. *beth* plus עוד (still) plus 3 f. s. suffix.

בכפו, prep. *beth* plus כַּף (double-*ayin* root, hence the doubled letter) plus 3 m. s. suffix. The root means 'be bent', hence כף is properly 'the bend of the hand, the hollow, the palm'.

יבלענה, 3 m. s. impf. qal plus *nun energicum* plus 3 f. s. suff. The root emphasizes the idea of speed, 'swallows it up, gulps it down'; cf. Jonah ii. 1.

Verse 5. צְפִירָה (chaplet). The root is צפר III, plait, braid. In Rabbinic Hebrew the word is used chiefly of the rim of a basket.

שְׁאָר (residue). The *qamets* is retained in the construct. According to GK 93*ww*, these forms are probably all loan-words from Aramaic. The word is Isaianic and late, as can be seen from a comparison of 1 Kings xi. 41 and 2 Chronicles ix. 29. It is advisable not to translate it by 'remnant', since the proper word for 'the Remnant' is שְׁאֵרִית.

Verse 6. The accentuation of MT, with *athnach* at מִשְׁפָּט, separates the first phrase from the rest. A better sense is obtained by the accentuation of four MSS. cited by Wickes (*Hebrew Prose Accents*, p. 74), which place the *athnach* at הַמִּשְׁפָּט. This latter is the rendering of LXX, V, and the English Versions, though S follows MT.

מְשִׁיבֵי, m. cstr. p. of hiph. ptc. of שׁוּב. All translations assume the insertion of the prep. *lamedh*, which seems to be necessary; so scholars generally. The whole phrase is difficult, and LXX seems to have read a different text. The general rendering is 'to those who turn back the battle from the gate', as in S. On the other hand, V and Douai have 'who turn back from the battle to the gate', which is שָׁבֵי מִמִּלְ'. The Targum takes the first part as referring to going out to battle and the final word as referring to returning home in peace.

שַׁעְרָה, 'to the gate', a toneless *he-locale*, DG 61*f*, WL 55 and 211, GK 90*c*.

Verse 7. וְגַם־אֵלֶּה, 'for even these'.

Both priest and prophet are cult-officials, connected with the local shrines, and each giving oracles in his own fashion. See article by Dr. A. R. Johnson, *Exp. Times*, April, 1936, pp. 317 *ff.*, 'The Prophet in Israelite Worship'. The author rightly draws a firm distinction between the cult-prophet and the canonical prophet.

בָּרֹאֶה, usually taken to mean 'in vision', but the word elsewhere means 'the seer'; cf. 1 Samuel ix. 9, etc.,

12

and there is no reason why this should not be the meaning here. All the cult officials of every kind have erred in company with each other.

פָּקוּ, 3 m. p. pf. qal of פּוּק I (reel, totter). In *ayin-vav* and double-*ayin* verbs the accent is usually retained in this form on the stem syllable, but there are a number of exceptions where the tone is on the last syllable, as is the rule with *lamedh-he* verbs. The reason for the present exception is probably to secure rhythmical uniformity, GK 72*l*.

פְּלִילִיָּה, only here. It means 'the giving of a decision'. The root had a probable original meaning 'interpose', whence it can mean either 'intercede' (e.g. תְּפִלָּה, 'prayer') or 'arbitrate, judge' (e.g. פְּלִילָה, 'an umpire's office'). Duhm, Kittel, and others would insert the prep. *beth*, but there is no need to introduce this, especially if the previous רֹאֶה be taken to mean 'seer'. Such a loose accusative is perhaps unusual, GK 118*g*, but it is certainly possible syntactically.

Verse 8. צֹאָה, 'filth', usually of human excrement, but here of drunkards' vomit. The word is in apposition to the previous word, further defining it, DS 41 (*e*), GK 131*c*.

בְּלִי, properly a substantive (lit. 'wearing out'), but in common use as an adverb of negation.

Verse 9. יוֹרֶה, 3 m. s. impf. hiph. of יָרָה. In qal the meaning is 'throw', but in hiphil 'throw, shoot (arrows), point out', and (as here) 'teach'. Here with two accusatives, of the person and the thing taught.

גְּמוּלֵי מֵחָלָב. This and the following constructs are both unusual, the pl. cstr. being followed by the prep. *min*, DS 37, GK 130*a*. The root גָּמַל means 'complete', and so 'to wean a child' is to complete his nursing. The following root עָתַק means 'move, advance', and so here 'removed from the breasts', unless perchance עַתִּיק is an Aramaism, and so the meaning is 'too old from the breasts', being used pregnantly.

שָׁדַיִם, dual form with qamets-with-silluq in pause at the end of the verse.

Verse 10. צַו, only here and Hosea v. 11 (command, precept). The meaning of the verse is uncertain, being a series of monosyllables. Ewald and Dillmann take it to mean the carpenter's rule and קַו as his line. Duhm and Cheyne take the words to be mocking words without any sense, but see Skinner's note in *Isaiah*, vol. i, p. 223.

לָצַו and לָקָו. Each with *qamets* twice, one with preposition in the pretone, and the other the tone vowel lengthened in pause. DG 51 and in part WL 45, GK 102*h*.

Verse 11. בְּלַעֲגֵי, prep. *beth* plus cstr. p. of לַעַג, 'stammerings of (lip)', i.e. in a foreign tongue; cf. the parallel phrase and the Greek βάρβαρος. So Ewald, and others, including Skinner and Whitehouse. The alternative is to assume that the absolute sing. is לַעַג, 'mocking', and so Delitzsch, Duhm, and Cheyne, but the word occurs only in Psalm xxxv. 16 and is doubtful. It is better to follow Ewald. On the strength of Isaiah xxxi. 4 (where LXX has ψελλίζουσαι). Graetz suggests עֹלְגֵי (speaking inarticulately), but the word is not found elsewhere, and MT may well stand.

יְדַבֵּר. S has the first person both here and in the following verse, whilst LXX has 3rd plural.

Verse 12. אֲשֶׁר וּבְ'. The English Versions follow the Vulgate *cui dixit* (to whom he said), but it is better to follow the other Versions and to translate, 'who said to them'.

הָנִיחוּ, 2 m. p. imperat. hiph. (first, and true hiphil; see verse 2) of נוּחַ; 'cause ye to rest'.

מַרְגֵּעָה, 'place of refreshing'. Found only here, but another form מַרְגּוֹעַ occurs once only at Jeremiah vi. 13. The root is רגע II, properly 'return to rest after wandering'. The root רגע I means 'disturb', and this is probably the explanation of the LXX σύντριμμα (affliction, ruin), a word apparently unknown in classical Greek.

אֲבוֹא. Some MSS. and Edd. have a Qere אבו, and some have אָבוּ, both Written and Read, but the true MT is beyond question אָבוֹא without a Qere. It is probably an early scribal error, GK 23*i*. The form is 3 p. pf. qal of אבה (be willing).

שְׁמוֹעַ, inf. cstr. qal without prep. *lamedh* after אבה. So nine times as against forty-one times with *lamedh*.

Verse 13. לְמַעַן is always 'in order that'. It is properly a preposition, and a conjunction only when followed by the relative, but when used as a conjunction the relative is most often omitted, and it is followed by the imperfect. The imperfect here is continued with a series of perfects with strong-*vav*.

וְנִשְׁבָּרוּ, *qamets* in pause with *zaqeph-qaton*, one of the lesser disjunctive accents, GK 29*i*. At the end of the verse, the same pausal vowel occurs with *silluq*.

וְנוֹקְשׁוּ, strong-*vav* plus 3 m. p. pf. niphal of יקשׁ (lay bait, set snare).

Verse 14. אַנְשֵׁי לָצוֹן, lit. 'men of scoffing'; cf. Proverbs xxix. 8. The phrase is equivalent to the לֵצִים (scoffers) of Psalm i. 1; men who deliberately make a mock of holy things, the most impious men of all.

Verse 15. חֹזֶה. The word means 'seer', and Hoffmann

would retain it (we think rightly) with this meaning, i.e. we have appointed a seer (necromancer) who will come to an agreement for us with the Underworld of the Dead. Duhm favours this interpretation, but would translate 'vision', obtained by necromancy. Some scholars would therefore read חָזוּת, as in verse 18; but we see no need to make a change, nor any need to translate 'vision' here any more than in the case of ראה in verse 7. The Versions seem all to have read MT, and they follow the Targum שְׁלָמָא (peace, agreement, e.g. the Vulgate *pactum*). They have probably been guided by the parallel phrase, and some such meaning is certain.

שׁיט. The Kethib is שִׁיט ('rowing', from the lashing of the water with the oar), and the Qere is שׁוֹט (scourge); which read.

שׁוֹטֵף (overflowing), and so the Versions except Theod., who reads שֶׁטֶף (κατακλυσμός, deluge). Targum has סָנְאָה (enemy), possibly paraphrasing, as often in this chapter. Duhm, Marti and others read שׁוֹטֵט (scourging). We agree with Skinner that this is no improvement, and it has no support in the Versions. The construction of the phrase is *casus pendens*, DS 148*ff*, DT 264. Translate 'the overflowing scourge, when it passes over (or, less good, "through"), it shall not attack us'. Cf. verse 18.

עבר. The Qere is יַעֲבֹר, the imperfect, see verse 18. The Kethib was the perfect, which might possibly stand; cf. Isaiah xvi. 12, and especially 1 Chronicles xvii. 11, which has been altered from the imperfect of 2 Samuel vii. 12.

יבואנו, 3 m. s. impf. qal plus 1 p. suffix; 'shall not

attack us'. Cf. Psalm xliv. 18. See BDB under בוא,
para. 2b (p. 98b).

מחסנו, the noun מַחְסֶה plus 1 p. suffix. LXX has
ἐλπίς (hope), and so seven times in the Psalms, and
so also Vulgate (spes).

Verse 16. יִסַּד, 3 m. s. pf. piel with *pathach* in second
syllable, as always (four times) with this form, GK 52l.
MT is difficult, 'Behold I, one has founded . . .' It
is better to follow the Versions and read יֹסֵד, act.
part. qal, translating as *fut. instans*, 'Behold I am about
to found . . .', DS 134, GK 116p. So most scholars.
Skinner would keep MT (cf. GK 155ƒ), and read
'Behold I am he that hath laid . . .', but it scarcely
seems possible to get this out of MT, though he has
some support in xxix. 14 and xxxviii. 5, where in both
cases most would read the participle.

אבן (first). Procksch, Kittel and others would omit,
partly on rhythmical grounds, and partly because
1 Peter ii. 6 omits it. Retain, since it is found in all
Versions except LXX, and that would account for
the omission in 1 Peter.

בחן ('testing'), only here and Ezekiel xxi. 18, where
most emend. The meaning is 'a tested stone', where-
fore many would read בָּחוּן, following Jewish tradition.
This is the pass. ptc. qal of the verb, which is easier,
though not strictly necessary. LXX, with ἐκλεκτόν, may
have read בחר. Gesenius-Kautzsch would make Zion
itself the foundation stone, explaining the preposition
as *beth essentiae*, GK 119i.

פנת וג', lit. 'a corner (stone) of preciousness of sure
foundation'. The adjective is used nominally and
brought into the string of constructs, DS 37 (Rem. 3);
GK 130ƒ (note 4) makes it a substantive.

17

מוּסָד. Kittel, Cheyne and others omit as dittograph. It is a 'barbarous' form, and is not found in 1 Peter ii. 6. Retain, for the sake of emphasis. The form is mixed, and is probably a combination of two traditional pronunciations, the hophal מוּסָד and מֻסָּד for the pual מְיֻסָּד.

הַמַּאֲמִין, article plus hiphil ptc., 'he that trusts'. Some LXX MSS. (not Cod. B) add ἐπ'αὐτῷ, an addition from 1 Peter ii. 6.

יָחִישׁ, 3 m. s. impf. hiph. of חוּשׁ, 'hasten away', but LXX has καταισχυνθῇ equals יֵבוֹשׁ (be ashamed), so Graetz and Procksch. Vulgate follows MT, but T and S have 'be terrified', whence Kittel suggests יָחִיל or יֵחַת, but most follow Duhm and Guthe, reading יָמוּשׁ (give way).

מִשְׁפָּט. For the meaning of this word and the following see my *Distinctive Ideas of the Old Testament*, pp. 74–7, 72–4.

לְקָו, 'as a line', the *lamedh* denoting the secondary predicate, WL 207 (para. *b*, v), GK 119*t*. LXX reads εἰς ἐλπίδα, i.e. לְתִקְוָה.

וְיָעָה strong-*vav* plus 3 m. s. pf. qal of יָעָה. The root means primarily 'sweep together', with a view to carrying away. The verb is found only here, but the meaning 'collect, gather' is found in Arabic. Cf. also the Hebrew יָע (shovel) for carrying away the refuse of the altar. LXX has a different text for 17*b*.

מַחְסֶה. Notice the *tsere* of the cstr. sing., the *seghol* belonging to the sing. absolute. Duhm and Cheyne would read the absolute here, and omit כָּזָב as being unnecessary. They thus obtain a more regular rhythmical structure. Such changes, in our view, are unwarranted, since we do not think that the Hebrew versification was always so precise.

יִשְׁטֹפוּ. The full vowel lost in the vocal *sheva* returns in pause as the tone vowel, DG 40*f*, WL 117, GK 29*m*.

Verse 18. וכפר, strong-*vav* plus 3 m. s. pf. pual of כפר (primarily 'cover over', and hence 'pacify, make propitiation'). Most scholars alter this to וְחֻפַּר, 'and shall be frustrated', but we agree with Skinner that there is no need for any change. It is true that this is the regular atonement word, but here it is used in its original meaning, 'shall be covered over', i.e. completely covered, so that it is no longer in sight.

וחזותכם, 'and your vision', i.e. that which the seer of verse 14 saw and declared as his oracle. LXX has 'hope' and Vulgate, S, 'agreement' (*pactum*). Note the retention of the *qamets*, GK 95*t*.

והייתם, strong-*vav* plus 2 m. p. pf. qal, acting as apodosis to the when-if clause. 'When it passes over, then ye shall be to it a trampling', DS 176, DT 174, GK 112*hh*. For the double use of *lamedh*, WL 207 para. (*b*) v.

Verse 19. מדי, prep. *min* plus cstr. of דַּי, a substantive meaning 'sufficiency, enough'. Lit. 'out of the abundance of its passing over', i.e. 'as often as . . .'

עָבְרוֹ, inf. cstr. qal plus 3 m. s. suffix; the first vowel is short-*o* followed by vocal *sheva*.

זועה. The word is a transposition from זְעָוָה (trembling, an object of trembling), from the root זוע. It occurs thrice in its true form, and five times as here, but in the other four cases (all in Jeremiah) the Qere is the true form.

הָבִין, inf. cstr. hiph. of בִּין (understand), used as a verbal noun, DG 77, DS 123, WL 100 (top), GK 114 a–c, 'and it shall be sheer terror to understand the report'. For רַק (only) with asserative force, see BDB p. 956b par. 2e.

Verse 20. מַצָּע (bed, couch). This form is found only here, the usual form being the poetical word יָצוּעַ. The root is the late יצע, a *pe-yod* verb which assimilates the *yod*.

מֵהִשְׂתָּרֵעַ. The prep. *min* is comparative, DG 161, WL 31f, GK 133a and c; cf. especially Isaiah l. 2. For the rest, the form is inf. cstr. hithp. of שׂרע, only here and twice in Leviticus xxi. 18, xxii. 23. The Arabic root means 'point directly at', whence the derived meaning 'extend', e.g. the stretched (and twisted) nose of the Vulgate in Leviticus xxi. 18. The sibilant and the dental have interchanged according to rule, DG 93, WL 72, GK 54b. Box, Cheyne, Procksch and Kuenen (doubtfully) omit the whole verse. The verse can well stand. The meaning is that the doom is fixed, and there is no escape. The simile is of a man on a pallet bed. The bed is too short for him to lie at full length, and if he draws up his knees, the coverlet is too narrow for him to keep himself covered.

מַסֵּכָה (coverlet). The root is נסך II, and means 'weave'.

צָרָה. The accent is on the first syllable, and so the form must be parsed as a verb and not as the adjective. 3 f. s. pf. qal of צרר I, used intransitively to mean 'to be narrow'. The *qamets* is to compensate for the impossibility of doubling the *resh*.

כְּהִתְכַּנֵּס, prep. *kaph* plus inf. cstr. hiph. of the root כנס (gather together). The synagogue is בֵּית הַכְּנֶסֶת (lit.

20

the house of gathering together). Most are agreed
that the *kaph* should be a *mem* as in 20*a*, but the *kaph*
can be retained (see BDB 488*a*), and translated, 'and
the covering too scant when he draws his feet up'.
Graetz read מֵהִתְכַּסּוֹת (for him to cover himself), but
this is not necessary. Vulgate (and Douai) evidently
did not understand the simile, and provided another
picture: 'for the bed is so narrow that one must fall
out, and a short covering cannot cover both'.

Verse 21. 'For as at Mount Perizim the Lord will
rise up, as in a vale in Gibeon He will rage, to do His
deed—alien is His deed; and to work His work—
foreign is His work.' Jehovah will fight as of old in
the Philistine wars, but now it will be against Israel'
as though He were an alien and a foreigner.

Verse 22. תתלוצצו, 2 m. p. impf. hithpolel of ליץ,
and meaning strictly, 'do not show yourself a scorner'.
Qamets under *zaqeph-qaton* in pause. אַל with the jussive
means 'don't'; לֹא with the imperfect, 'thou shalt not',
DG 83, WL 85 and 77, DS 88 and 86, GK 107*o*.

יחזקו. This root has the sense of a firm, strong grip.

מוסריכם, 2 m. p. suffix to plural of מוֹסֵר, a third
declension form from the root אסר (bind).

כלה ונחרצה, as in Isaiah x. 23 and Daniel ix. 27.
'A complete destruction and a clear-cut (decisive)
decision.' The first word is a substantive, and the
second is f. s. niph. ptc. of חרץ I (cut, sharpen),
though Barth makes it an inf. cstr.

אדני. Not in 4 Heb. MSS., S, LXX. Cheyne omits,
and it may well be a conflation.

על־כל־הארץ. Duhm and Cheyne omit this as over-
burdening the metre.

Verse 24. כל היום. Comes first after the inter-

21

rogative, as being the important element. 'Does he *continually* plough, etc.?'

יחרש, 3 m. s. impf. qal of חרש I (cut in, engrave, plough). Imperfect of actions customary, DS 66, DT 38, GK 107*f, g*.

לזרע. Most scholars omit this as a gloss, probably correctly.

וישׂדד, weak *vav* (the two actions are coincident rather than consecutive) plus 3 m. s. imf. piel of שׂדד with *sin*. Elsewhere only Hosea x. 11; Job xxxix. 10, but it was doubtless a common enough word, and the regular word for 'harrow'. The vocal-*sheva* under the *yod* has coalesced before the weak *vav* into a long *chireq*, as usually, DG 53, WL 44, GK 24*b*.

Verse 25. הלוא אם. 'Is it not the case that when he shall have . . ., then he will scatter . . . and will toss. . . .' The אם here means almost 'when' (see BDB 50*a* bottom). Cf. the Latin future perfect in the protasis, and the future in the apodosis, DS 177, DT 178*f*, WL 206 (2 Samuel xv. 33), GK 106*o*. Here we have perfect in the protasis, followed by perfect with strong-*vav*.

כמן, 'cummin'. All three letters belong to the root.

יזרק. This root strictly means 'toss abundantly, in handfuls', as against the previous פוץ I, which properly is 'disperse'.

חטה. The singular refers to wheat in the ear (all together in the field), and חטים, the plural, to wheat in grain. Similarly שׂערה (barley) and שׂערים, and כֻּסֶּמֶת (spelt) and כֻּסְּמִים, DS 19 (Rem. 1), GK 124*m*. The prophet is thinking of the corn standing in the field, rather than of the actual seed that is being sown.

שׂורה. Not in LXX, S. There is general agreement

22

that it is a miswritten dittograph of the following word. V and EVV have 'in rows', but in this case the first letter should be *sin* and not *shin*. If the word is omitted, then 'the wheat and the barley' form one half of the line, and what follows belongs to the second half.

נִסְמָן. Presumably the niphal ptc. of a root סמן, not otherwise known in OT, but used in the Talmud as a denominative of סִימָן (mark). If the reading is sound, the word must mean 'in the marked (appointed) place', but this meaning is neither natural to the Hebrew, nor is it readily intelligible. It is best omitted as a dittograph, and so Wellhausen, Duhm, Cheyne, Box, and Skinner. It is not in LXX, though Cod. B has καί κέγχρον, as Aq. and Theod. This word stands for דֹּחַן (millet) in Ezekiel iv. 9, so that probably the Greek Versions, finding an unintelligible word, considered it to be the name of another cereal, and filled in on the strength of the other passage.

Verse 26. וַיִּסְּרוֹ, strong-*vav* plus 3 m. s. pf. piel of יסר (discipline, admonish, instruct). Most scholars insert יהוה, which helps both the rhythm and the sense. Kennicott has pointed out that at a very early date the Sacred Name was indicated by י׳. Kissane suggests יָקֶב, and connects it with 25*d*, 'and with millet and spelt he surrounds his border'. The Versions evidently read much the same text, though LXX and S read the last word of the verse with *daleth* instead of *resh*, e.g. S has 'God will instruct him in judgement, and he will praise him'. Cf. the LXX εὐφρανθῆσῃ, i.e. יוֹדֶנּוּ.

מִשְׁפָּט here means 'established custom'; see BDB 1049*a*.

Verse 27. בְּחָרוּץ, prep. *beth* plus article plus חרוץ, properly an adjective meaning 'sharp', here used as a substantive without מוֹרַג; cf. xli. 15. The article is used of the particular instrument which the husbandman is envisaged as using, DS 26, GK 126*d*.

יוּדַשׁ, 3 m. s. impf. hoph. of דּוּשׁ (thresh). The imperfect of custom, DS 66, DT 38, GK 107*g*, and so throughout this verse and the next. The tone has been retracted to avoid the concurrence of two tone syllables, GK 29*e*.

אוֹפַן (wheel), cstr. sing. The *nun* is doubled with suffixes, DG 141, WL 55, GK 93*ee*.

יוּסָּב, 3 m. s. imf. hoph. of סבב (surround, turn about) with *qamets* for *pathach* in the final syllable in pause with *athnach*. The *vav* 'full' is unusual before the *dagesh* in double-*ayin* verbs, the custom being to have either a short vowel and *dagesh* or a long vowel without *dagesh*. The composite form here is demanded by the Masora.

Verse 28. The verse can scarcely stand as it is, since the last two words contradict the first two. Either make the first two a question, or omit them altogether as a gloss. The former is better, either with or without the interrogative *he*, and so scholars generally. There is no justification in OT for translating the root דקק as 'thresh'. The word means 'pulverize, crush into dust'. The only possible case, apart from this verse, is Isaiah xli. 15, where the ordinary word 'thresh', דּוּשׁ, is used in a figurative sense of 'pulverize' as a parallel to דקק, and not vice versa. 'Is bread (-corn) crushed? No, he does not keep threshing it for ever.' For the use of כִּי in this negative sense, see BDB p. 474*a* (bottom), otherwise it is causal.

24

יוּדָּק, 3 m. s. imf. hoph. of double-*ayin* root, with *qamets* for *pathach* in pause with *zaqeph-qaton*.

אדוֹשׁ. It is best to follow the Targum and Vulgate, and read דּוֹשׁ, inf. abs. qal, as intensifying the following finite verb, DG 77, WL 101, DS 117, GK 113*n*. Koenig suggested the word means 'thresher', presumably with *aleph* prosthetic, GK 19*m*, 85*b*, or alternatively that it is part of a gloss 'not always will I thresh', since it could be 1 s. imf. qal. Procksch suggests אֱנוֹשׁ, but the Targum is best. LXX has a different and much shorter text.

יְדוּשֶׁנּוּ, 3 m. s. imf. qal plus *nun energicum* plus 3 m. s. suffix.

וְהָמַם, strong-*vav* plus 3 m. s. pf. qal of הָמַם (move noisily), continuing from the previous verse, 'and he rolls his wagon wheel (over it)'.

וּפָרָשָׁיו. The conjunction *vav* becomes *shureq* before the labial, DG 53, WL 44, GK 26*a*. The *qamets* under *pe* is firm, since it stands for *pathach* with following *dagesh*, the formation denoting occupation, GK 84*b*b. Graetz, Cheyne substitute וְהָרוּצוֹ on the ground that a separate mention of the horses (*sic*) is not necessary. Duhm and others read וּפְרָשׂוֹ וְלֹא, 'and he spreads it out without crushing it'. V (*ungulis suis*), S, Sym., Theod. have read פְּרָשָׁיו, as if פְּרָסָיו (with his hoofs). It is best to follow Duhm. MT reads 'and he rolls his wagon wheel over it and his horsemen: he does not pulverize it'.

יְדֻקֶּנּוּ, 3 m. s. imf. qal of double-*ayin* root plus *nun energicum* plus 3 m. s. suffix.

Verse 29. יָצְאָה, 3 f. s. pf. qal, with the original *qamets* under *tsade* returning in pause with *athnach*, DG 40, WL 117, GK 29*m*.

25

הפליא וג', lit. 'He makes-wonderful counsel; He makes-great insight'. Both nouns are technical terms in Wisdom Literature. The line may well be a post-exilic addition.

CHAPTER XXIX

Verse 1. אריאל. A name applied to Jerusalem, meaning either 'lion of El' or 'altar of El'. The Targum has מַדְבְּחָא, 'O altar', which Cheyne suggested was originally מזבח י', i.e. 'altar of the Lord'. The meaning 'hearth of El' is the more satisfactory explanation, in view both of verse 2, 'and she shall be unto me as a (real) Ariel', i.e. a place of ashes, reeking with the blood of human victims (cf. Skinner), and of line 12 of the Moabite Stone, where the phrase אראל דודה (altar-hearth of David?) is found. See EB, HDB, and the commentaries.

קרית, cstr. sing. of קִרְיָה, before the clause 'David encamped', DS 21, 35, GK 130*d*. This noun ('city') is found in the names Carthage, Carthagena.

ספו. See GK 69*h* (note). 2 m. p. imperat. qal of יסף (add), occurring here and Jeremiah vii. 21. The Masoretes seem to have envisaged a root ספה; cf. their pointing, לִסְפּוֹת, in Numbers xxxii. 14 and סְפוֹת in Isaiah xxx. 1, where we would expect (לְסֶפֶת).

חַגִּים. Notice the *dagesh* denoting the double-*ayin* root. Cf. the Arabic *chajj* of the pilgrimage feast to Mecca. The reference here is not to the three agricultural pilgrimages of the Hebrew-Canaanite year, but to the great Feast of Asiph (Ingathering), which marked the end of one year and the beginning of the next.

ינקפו, 3 m. p. impf. qal of נקף II (go around), with the *nun* retained (rare), GK 66*f*. The tone is retracted in pause with *silluq* at the end of the sentence, and the original -*o* reappears, DG 40, WL 117, GK 29*m*.

Verse 2. והציקותי, strong-*vav* plus 1 s. pf. hiph. of קוץ (press upon, bring into straits), following on the previous sentence as a natural sequence, DS 82, DT 152, GK 112*x*.

והיתה, 'and there shall come to be'. This Hebrew root does not mean 'to be' so much as 'to come to be'.

תאניה ואניה. These two parallel forms from the root אנה I (mourn) occur twice only and together, here and Lamentations ii. 5. Cheyne, to preserve the assonance, 'moaning and bemoaning'.

והיתה לי, 'and she shall be to me . . .', but this is unlikely, since it gives two different uses for והיתה in close conjunction. It is better to follow, as do most, Duhm's suggestion and read the 2nd pers. fem. וְהָיִית לִי, 'and thou shalt be to me'. Note the euphonic *dagesh* in the *lamedh*, which is due to the retraction of the tone, leaving a toneless -*ah*, GK 20*f*. The retraction is to avoid the concurrence of two accented syllables; cf. xxviii. 7.

Verse 3. כַּדּוּר, 'like a circle', with the article in a comparison, i.e. the particular circle of which the author is thinking, GK 126*o*. So V and T, but LXX read כְּדָוִד (like David), and many scholars accept this. Targum has מַשְׁרְיָן (camps), reading probably some derivative of the root דּוּר (dwell: cf. Psalm lxxxiv. 11). According to Jastrow, there is a word כַּדּוּר, meaning 'circle, cordon'; cf. Assyrian *kuduru*. The word is frequent in the Talmud in the sense of 'circle, ball', and the hithpael of the verb is used in *Qoheleth Rabba* of a ball being thrown round in a circle. It is probably best, therefore, to retain MT and to translate, 'and I will encamp in a cordon against thee'.

וְצַרְתִּי, strong-*vav* plus 1 s. pf. qal of צוּר II (bind, besiege), here with an accusative 'pallisade'. The tone has been advanced to the last syllable, according to the regular custom in the 1st and 2nd singular, DG 85 (bottom), GK 49*h–l*. The note at WL 90 is inadequate. For an explanation of this phenomenon see G. R. Driver, *Problems of the Hebrew Verbal System* (1936), pp. 85–97, where he finds the origin in tenses comparable to the Accadian preterite and permansive tenses, a suggestion which has much to recommend it. There is no need to read וְצִוִּיתִי, 'I have commanded'.

מצב (palisade, entrenchment), found only here, a derivative from the root נצב (set up, erect). The parallel is מצרת, from the root צוּר II, having the same meaning.

Verse 4. תדברי, 2 f. s. impf. piel, with the original *tsere* returning in pause with *zaqeph-qaton*.

תשח, 3 f. s. imf. niph. of שחח (bow, be bowed down), i.e. 'and thy speech shall proceed humbly from the dust'. The verse proceeds, 'and thy voice shall be like a ghost out of the ground, and from the dust thy speech shall chirp', the last word being 3 f. s. impf. pilpel of צפף.

Verse 5. כאבק דק, 'like powdered dust'. The article, usually found in comparisons with the prep. *kaph*, is regularly omitted when a qualifying adjective or clause is used, the idea being that the qualification itself makes the comparison sufficiently definite, GK 126*p*. LXX extends the simile to the dust cloud raised by a wheel.

המון, cstr. s. of הָמוֹן from the root המה (murmur, growl, roar), whence the noun means 'sound, murmuring', and thence 'crowd, multitude' as causing the noise. LXX understands the word in its late sense, 'abundance'.

זריך, 'thy strangers' (as AV), or 'aliens', but it is best to follow RV with 'thy adversaries', i.e. צָרָיִךְ. So most. LXX has 'ungodly', probably reading זֵדָיִךְ. Vulgate has *ventilantium te*, 'of those that fan thee', reading זָרָיִךְ from the root זרה.

עריצים. Notice the firm *qamets* in the first syllable. The ground form is *pathach* with following *dagesh* to denote people in possession of a quality in an intensive manner, GK 84^b f. The root means 'tremble', so translate 'the terrible ones'. It is best to end the verse here, so that 5*c* can go with 6*a*.

פתאם, properly a noun meaning 'suddenness' as פתע, with the *ayin* weakened to *aleph*. Kittel suggests שָׁאוֹן (uproar), on the basis of the Targum אִתְרְגוּשָׁא, but this is not necessary, since two adverbs from the same root are found together, GK 133*k* (note on p. 432).

Verse 6. תפקד, 3 f. s. impf. niph. If it were 'thou' (2 f. s.), it would have to be תִּפָּקְדִי.

רעם. Procksch would omit this and the following *vav*. It may be redundant, but by no means necessarily so.

אוכלה, f. s. act. pts. qal. This form with the original short -*i* lengthened into *tsere* instead of shortened into *sheva*, occurs (chiefly in pause) some eight times altogether, and generally with fem. substantives of this form, GK 84^{a}s. There is another case in verse 8, where it is in pause with *athnach*.

C   29

Verse 7. הצבאים, art. plus m. p. act. ptc. qal, 'those who are mustering for war'. The noun צָבָא means the militia, called up in time of war, every able-bodied man, and distinct from the bodyguard, the small standing army of foreign mercenaries which, for instance, Benaiah commanded in David's time.

צביה. Difficult and doubtful. Presumably it is m. p. act. ptc. qal of צבא, but entirely as if a *lamedh-he* verb plus 3 f. s. suffix, GK 75*qq*. If so, the meaning is 'all those of her that are mustering', but we are now in another section and the doom is upon the enemies of Israel. The sense intended is that of the EVV, but they cannot stand as a translation of the Hebrew, though they follow the tradition of the Versions. It is best to follow Duhm and Box, who read מַצְּבֵיהֶם וּמְצָרְתֵיהֶם, 'their entrenchments and their siege-works' (cf. verse 3), unless we make both into singulars, as Procksch and Skinner.

והמציקים, copula plus article plus m. p. ptc. hithp. of צִיק I (press upon, distress).

Verse 8. הרעב, with the article to denote the particular hungry man who is present to the mind of the speaker, DS 26, GK 126*q-s*.

הנה, followed by the ptc. without the article, which is unusual, GK 116*s*.

והקיץ, strong-*vav* plus 3 m. s. pf. hiph. of קִיץ I (awake), following on יחלם; 'and it shall be as when a hungry man dreams . . . and awakes. . . .'

וריקה נפשו, 'and his *nephesh* is empty', i.e. his longing for food is still unsatisfied. Cf. xxxii. 6, 'to keep empty the hungry *nephesh*'. This word should never be translated 'soul'. It is the seat of the appetites and desire, and here is better rendered 'longing'.

Verse 9. התמהמהו, 2 m. p. imperat. hithpalpel of
מהה (linger, tarry), a double-*ayin* verb and not *lamedh-*
he, GK 55*g*. Most scholars, however, read, following
the Versions, הִתַּמְּהוּ, 2 m. p. imperat. hithp. of תמה (be
ye astounded), the same root as the following verb, and
so RVm. This is probably correct, in view of the
following phrase, where we have the hithpalpel of שעע
(be blind) followed by the qal of the same root. See
also Habakkuk i. 5. The *tau* of the preformative is
assimilated to the following *t*-sound, DG 93, WL 72,
GK 54*c*.

השתעשעו, 2 m. p. imperat. hithpalpel of שעע I,
followed by 2 m. p. imperat. qal of the same root,
'blind yourselves and be blind' as in RVm. The *shin*
and the *tau* change places according to rule, DG 93,
WL 72, GK 54*b*. Buhl suggests הִשְׁתָּעוּ וּשְׁעוּ, hithpael
and qal of the root שעה (gaze steadily), i.e. 'gaze about
and gaze (in anxiety)'; cf. xli. 10, 23.

שכרו, 3 p. pf. qal of שכר (be drunken). Commentators follow LXX, and read the imperative שִׁכְרוּ,
and so also for the following verb, making it נֻעוּ,
2 m. p. imperat. qal of נוע (totter, stagger). The latter
verb has no equivalent in LXX.

Verse 10. רוח, i.e. overpowering spirit. The word
carries with it the idea of power, and, as a psycho-
logical term, is used to denote dominating disposition,
e.g. Genesis xxvi. 35; Numbers v. 14, 30.

תרדמה is properly the deep sleep occasioned by the
approach of Deity, Genesis ii. 21; Job iv. 13; etc. It is
an insensibility of supernatural origin.

ויעצם, strong-*vav* plus 3 m. s. impf. piel of עצם II
(shut the eyes), only here and xxxiii. 15.

את־הנביאים and חזים are both generally recognized

as glosses, though both are found in the Versions. The reference of the prophet was not to any particular functionaries, but to the people as a whole. The sign of the accusative את need not be repeated unless the first of the two nouns in apposition is personal, DS 40, GK 131*h*.

חזות הכל. Not 'all vision', but the vision of the whole group of visionary seers.

הספר, properly a scroll. The article is used to denote the particular scroll in the mind of the speaker; cf. verse 8. When the word occurs the second time, it is better to follow the Qere and omit the article. On the other hand, the Kethib may intend to refer to the particular man who was able to read the scroll.

קרא, 2 m. s. imperat. qal, properly 'read aloud'.

אוכל, 1 s. impf. qal of יָכֹל (be able), DG 129, WL 138, GK 69*r*.

Verse 12. ונתן, strong-*vav* plus 3 m. s. pf. niph. of נתן following on the impf. יתנו of the previous verse —'which they give to a man who can read . . . and then the scroll is given to . . .'.

על. Read אֶל, as in LXX.

ידע and ידעתי are both perfects showing the state of mind as due to pre-existing conditions, DG 156, DS 60, DT 16, GK 106*g*.

Verse 13. אדני. Retain. It is one of the 134 cases, according to the Masora, where this stands for the Tetragrammaton.

יען כי and יען אשר are the most common causal conjunctions, DS 198, GK 158*b*.

נִגַּשׁ, 3 m. s. pf. niph. of נגשׁ (draw near), here of worship.

בפיו, prep. *beth* plus פֶּה (mouth) plus 3 m. s. suffix, DG 153, WL 176, GK 96. MT reads, 'in as much as this people has drawn near, with their mouth and with their lips they have honoured me', as RV, but it is better to transfer the *zaqeph-qaton* from the previous word, and to follow the translation of AV, which, in its turn, follows LXX (Cod. B), V and S, i.e. 'has drawn near with their mouth, and with their lips . . .'. Procksch would omit the word and with it the following *vav*, this following the other major LXX MSS.

כבדוני, 3 m. p. pf. piel plus 1 s. suff. Duhm, Cheyne, Procksch and others read the sing. כִּבְּדָנִי, but the change is not necessary, though syntactically it is more correct.

לבו. For the use of this word לֵב (double-*ayin* noun) and the word לֵבָב (first declension), referring to the heart as the central core of man's being, and not of the mind only, see BDB under both words. There is no distinction between the two words, and the choice is a matter of style or even of caprice.

רִחַק, 3 m. s. pf. piel of רחק (to be, become far distant), 'their heart they have removed far away', as EVV, but the Versions have 'their heart is (or "has come to be") far away', reading either the pf. qal of the verb (has come to be far away) or the adjective רָחֹק (is far away). The former is preferable, in view of following note. Note that the *tsere* of the final syllable of the piel has become *pathach* under influence of the guttural, and also that the first vowel has not been lengthened to *tsere* to compensate for the doubled guttural. This is normal when the medial guttural is *he*, *cheth*, or *ayin*, DG 120, WL 177, GK 64*e*.

ותהי, strong-*vav* plus 3 f. s. impf. (apoc.) qal of היה, here used in its true sense of 'come to be'. For apocopation, see DG 148, WL 145, GK 75*s*. LXX has

33

'in vain do they worship me, teaching the command-
ments of men, and doctrines', whence Matthew xv. 9.
This involves reading the first word as וְתֹהוּ.

יראתם, inf. cstr. qal of יָרֵא (fear) plus 3 m. p. suff.,
'and their fearing (i.e. worshipping, LXX, σέβονται)
me has come to be . . .'. The inf. cstr. qal of a *pe-yod*
verb is liable to be unusual, and each verb needs to be
noted particularly.

מלמדה, f. s. ptc. pual, agreeing with 'command-
ment'. T makes the ptc. agree with 'men', מְלַמְּדִים,
V has 'and doctrines', whilst LXX has a compromise
of both, and so S.

Verse 14. יוֹסִף, 3 m. s. impf. hiph. of יסף. If correct,
the translation is 'Behold I, who will again . . .',
GK 155*f*; cf. note on xxviii. 16. We should probably
read יוֹסֵף the qal participle, 'behold I will again . . .',
and this is what the EVV have assumed. For the use
of this verb with following *lamedh* and inf. cstr. meaning 'I will again . . .', DG 129, WL 138, DS 114,
GK 120*d*.

את־העם־הזה. Omit. They spoil both sense and
rhythm. A clear case where the metrical theorist is
right.

הַפְלֵא, inf. abs. hiph., the second half of the line
meaning 'to do exceeding wonderfully and won-
drously'. The inf. abs. here perforce follows the
verb, but it has the idea of emphasis, DS 118 (bottom),
GK 113*r*. Sometimes its place is taken by the abstract
noun from the same root, but here both occur uniquely,
DS 120 (top), GK 113*w*.

תסתתר, 3 f. s. impf. hithpael of סתר (hide, secrete),
with *qamets* in pause for the normal *pathach*, which

34

itself was due to the final *resh*. *Tau* and *samech* interchange according to rule, DG 93, WL 72, GK 54*b*. Translate 'shall hide himself carefully'.

Verse 15. הַמַּעֲמִיקִים, article plus m. p. ptc. hiph. of intransitive verb עָמֹק: lit. 'those who make deep to hide', i.e. who deliberately hide deeply, DS 114, GK 120*a*.

לַסְתִּר, prep. *lamedh* plus inf. cstr. hiph. with *he* elided, GK 53*q*, but Cheyne and others would read the piel inf. cstr. לְסַתֵּר. There is no need to change. Duhm thinks something should be introduced to describe the doom of the apostates.

וְהָיָה, pf. with strong-*vav* following the participle, and followed by an impf. with strong-*vav*. Both are sound, the first strong-*vav* hurriedly interpolating a fact in the main statement. The meaning is that they keep on concealing counsel from God and so their deeds are in darkness, and then they say . . ., DT 138 (obs.). Procksch would delete the last verb.

בְמַחְשָׁךְ, prep. *beth* plus substantive in the absolute, 'in a dark (secret) place'. The final vowel is *qamets*, and not *pathach*, as in BDB and Baer's text. So also in xl. 16.

רֹאֵנוּ, act. qal ptc. רֹאֶה plus 1 p. suff., translated correctly by the English present tense, and similarly for the following verb.

Verse 16. הַפְכְּכֶם, noun הֶפֶךְ (perversity) plus 2 m. p. suff., 'Oh your perversity', DS 162, GK 147*c*. Some Bibles, notably Michaelis 1720, the two Athias Bibles of 1661 and 1667, and the Letteris (Bible Society) Bible, have *qamets chaṭuph* under the *he*, but the true Masoretic reading is *pathach*. Procksch would prefix הוֹי.

אִם וג'. One of the rare cases where a *simple* question

35

is introduced by אִם, GK 150*f*, where it is suggested that in the four cases there cited, the first member of the double question has been suppressed. It is better here to regard the previous word as taking the place of the first question. Vulgate has *quasi si*, i.e. the Douai 'as if . . .'

כְּחֹמֶר הַיֹּצֵר. The translation of MT is 'Shall he (it) be reckoned as the potter's clay', parsing חֹמֶר as cstr. sing.; cf. LXX. The passage has been misunderstood in Jewish tradition from ancient times, the accents being *merkha* and *tiphkha*, which link the two words together. The proper meaning is obtained by reading the accents *tiphkha* and *merkha*, and then translating, 'Shall the potter be counted as the clay?', and this is what the EVV have done. Vulgate and Douai follow the accents of MT, but read the following verb as qal, 'as if the clay should think against the potter', though this can scarcely be got out of the Hebrew.

לְעֹשֵׂהוּ, prep. *lamedh* plus m. s. act. ptc. qal plus 3 m. s. suff. The prep. is used as a 'dative of reference', DS 140, WL 207 (top), GK 119*u*, 'that what is made should say of him that made it, He did not make me'.

עָשָׂנִי, 3 m. s. pf. qal of עָשָׂה (make, do) plus 1 s. suff. Notice the *qamets* under the *sin*. This is in pause under *zaqeph-qaton* for the normal *pathach*; cf. the grammars and GK 175*ll*.

Verse 17. מִזְעָר, 'a little while', following and further limiting the preceding substantive מְעַט (a few). This apposition construction is good idiomatic Hebrew, and should be carefully studied, DS 39–41, GK 131*a*.

וְשָׁב, pf. with strong-*vav*, following an understood future verb, DS 82 (par. 56), DT 139, GK 112*x*, 'and Lebanon shall turn to Carmel'.

36

לכרמל, 'to garden land (or to Carmel), and Carmel shall be reckoned as forest (i.e. the rocky bad-lands)'. It is often difficult to know whether הברמל means Mount Carmel (lit. 'the Carmel') or 'any particular (garden land)' present to the mind of the writer. Here the exegesis is difficult. See the commentaries, and especially Skinner, *Isaiah*, vol. i, p. 236. The commentators who interpret יער (forest) to imply 'rich luxuriance' are sadly at fault, from Qimchi onwards. Note also the use of the article, which is usual with Carmel, Lebanon, and Jordan.

Verse 18. החרשים, article plus m. p. of adj. חֵרֵשׁ (dumb, deaf). The normal form expressing physical disability is עִוֵּר (blind); cf. in the next line, GK 84^{a}d. Here the root is חרשׁ II, and the usual *chireq* has been lengthened to *tsere* because the *resh* cannot be doubled. The *tsere* is therefore firm, and the adj. is third declension.

עורים, m. p. of עִוֵּר (blind). The *dagesh* has failed in the *vav* because of the vocal *sheva*, DG 33, WL 20, GK 20*m*.

Verse 19. ענוים, m. p. of עָנָו (humble, poor), this being an 'active' adj. from the root ענה III, just as עָנִי (afflicted poor) is the 'passive' adjective. Both adjectives come to be used specially, and sometimes technically, for humble, afflicted Israel, the faithful Remnant; cf. Psalm xxxvii. 11 and its dependent Matthew v. 5.

ביהוה. Procksch would delete this, but if we are going to find any strict rule of metre in this verse, many more deletions must be made, as indeed Procksch does.

אביוני, m. cstr. pl. followed by a partitive genitive.

This is equivalent to a superlative 'and the poorest of men', DG 161, WL 32, GK 133*h*.

Verse 20. אָפֵס, 3 m. s. pf. qal (cease, come to an end), not a common verb, though the noun אֶפֶס derived from this root is very common as a particle of negation in verse and exalted prose. The perfect is a perfect of certainty, DS 61, DT 20, GK 106*n*, and in English is 'shall certainly cease'. It is not enough to use the ordinary English future, any more than it was enough for the prophet to use the Hebrew imperfect.

וְכָלָה. This is perfect with weak-*vav*, the two phrases being synonymous, DS 84, DT 159, GK 154*a*, but in view of the following וְנִכְרְתוּ (which is certainly strong-*vav*) it might be taken to be perfect with strong-*vav*, following a 'perfect of certainty' regarded as a future, DT 126. It is better to take the first as a weak-*vav* since the two actions are contemporaneous, and then to take וְנִכְרְתוּ to be perfect with strong-*vav*, since that action may be regarded as the sequel to the two former actions. Note the retraction of the tone in כָלָה, in order to prevent the immediate concurrence of two accented syllables, DG 41, WL 117*f*, GK 29*e*.

שֹׁקְדִי, m. cstr. p. of act. ptc. qal of שָׁקַד (watch, wake); cf. Jeremiah i. 11, of the almond as 'the waker-tree'. LXX has οἱ ἀνομοῦντες, 'they that transgress', reading the root שֶׁקֶר.

Verse 21. מַחֲטִיאֵי, m. cstr. pl. of ptc. hiph., not here in ethical or religious sense of 'make to err, sin', but juridical 'make to be an offender by a (false) word'.

יְקֹשׁוּן, 3 m. p. impf. qal of קוֹשׁ (lay bait, lure), only here, and presumably a parallel form of the more usual יָקֹשׁ; cf. GK 72*r*. Note that BDB gives קוֹשׁ, but it

should be קֹשׁ with *cholem*. Kittel would correct to
יְקֹשׁוּ, by which presumably he intends the m. p.
impf. qal in pause of יקשׁ, but this should be יְקֹשׁוּ,
since the original vowel here also is *cholem*. The
ending here is in -*un* and bearing the tone, this being
the old original ending surviving regularly in Arabic
and Aramaic, and in Hebrew for emphasis and in
pause, as here, DG 77 (top), WL 77, GK 47*m*.

וַיֵּט, strong-*vav* plus 3 m. p. imf. hiph. of נטה (in-
cline), DG 151*f*, WL 144 (hiph., not hoph.), GK 76*c*.
This construction is strange following the previous
impf., but see previous note.

בתהו, 'with a thing of nought' as RV, and not
'for . . .', as AV.

Verse 22. אל־בית. This can scarcely be 'to the house
of Jacob' because of the following relative clause. The
EVV transfer the relative clause and understand על
(concerning). Lowth, Duhm, Cheyne, and most
scholars read אֵל, 'the God of the house of Jacob'.
Dillmann objected to this on the ground that it is not
Isaianic, but that is probably true of the whole section
from verse 15, though verse 16 might belong to the
prophet himself.

אשר וג'. This relative clause is difficult, first of all
because of its position, and secondly because of the
doubtful reference, unless perchance the section is
exilic and under the influence of Deutero-Isaiah. Paul
Reuben cleverly suggested אשר פדה אתו בְּרֶחֶם, 'whom
he redeemed in the womb'. Cheyne improved the
suggestion with מֵרֶחֶם (from the womb). Some scholars
adopt this tentatively, though others excise the whole
clause. It is probably best to regard it as an early
gloss.

יבוש, 3 m. s. impf. qal of stative verb בּוֹשׁ (to be ashamed).

יחורו, 3 m. p. impf. qal of חָוַר (to grow white, pale), not an *ayin-verb*. Verb found only here, but the piel form is common in Rabbinic Hebrew in the sense of 'make evident, clear'. Notice the effect of the pause in restoring the *chateph seghol* under the guttural, the normal form being יֶחֱוָרוּ. The Versions all reproduce the correct sense, though Theod. with ἐντραπήσεται may have read יֶחְפָּרוּ (shall be abashed). This is the root found in S, and many scholars adopt this more usual word instead of the unique verb in the text. LXX and T have 'change countenanc⸗', whilst V has *erubescet* (blush), but these may all be free renderings of MT.

Verse 23. בראתו, prep. *beth* plus inf. cstr. qal of ראה (see) plus 3 m. s. suff., 'but when he (Jacob) sees his children, the work of my hands, in his midst . . .', a passage which is not as difficult as is generally thought, if it is taken as belonging to the same set of circumstances as xlix. 14–25.

ילדיו. Generally agreed to be a gloss, some say on the suffix of the previous word, but Cheyne is sounder when he suggests that it is on the following phrase.

מעשׂה. Notice the *tsere*, which is the sign here of the construct, the absolute being with *seghol*.

שׁמי. Noun שֵׁם (name) plus 1 s. suffix, DG 153, WL 186, GK 96 (p. 284).

יעריצו. The hiphil of this root has two meanings, 'treat with awe' (as here) and 'inspire with awe' as viii. 13.

CHAPTER XXX

Verse 1. סוֹרְרִים, m. p. act. ptc. qal of סרר (be stubborn, rebellious). The root סוּר means 'turn aside', and has no immediate connection. The Douai 'apostates' is good.

נְאֻם. This word is now usually explained as the cstr. s. of a noun meaning 'utterance', but was previously regarded as the m. cstr. s. pass. ptc. of the verb. The usual translation is 'Oracle of the Lord', taken either as an introductory call, or as an interpolation into the actual matter of the prophecy. The proper significance of the word is given in GK 50*a* (note), with 'whispering', the corresponding Arabic root meaning 'groan, sigh'. It is the message which God 'whispers' to the prophet alone, which he then speaks forth under Divine compulsion.

מֶנִּי, prep. *min* plus 1 s. suff. This form occurs four times only, and six times in pause in the form מֶ֫נִּי, for the usual מִמֶּ֫נִּי, GK 103*i*.

לִנְסֹךְ מַסֵּכָה, 'to pour out libations' as the conclusion of an agreement, as LXX has seen. On the other hand, V, Aq. and Douai refer to the weaving of a web, taking both noun and verb to be נסך II as against נסך I. If it be argued that the noun מַסֵּכָה is never elsewhere used to mean 'libation', it can be replied that the verb is never used elsewhere 'to weave'. It seems best therefore to take the passage to refer to the treaty recently made with Egypt, rather than to the ungodly plots of the politicians.

מפות. This form strictly is inf. cstr. qal from a root
ספה, but it is better to read סְפֵת, inf. cstr. qal of יסף
(add). See GK 69*h* (note) and the note above on
xxix. 1.

Verse 2. לרדת, prep. *lamedh* plus inf. cstr. qal of ירד
(go down), one of the six *pe-yod* verbs like יֵשֵׁב. Tone-
long *qamets* in the pretone, DG 51, WL 45, GK 102*f*.

מצרים, dual form, lit. 'the two Egypts', i.e. Upper
and Lower Egypt.

ופי, conjunction *vav*, but *shureq* before labial, DG 53,
WL 44, GK 26*e*; followed by פֶּה (mouth) with 1 s.
suff., DG 153, WL 186, GK 96. LXX has 'me' instead of 'my mouth', whilst T interprets as 'the words
of the prophets'.

שאלו, 3 p. pf. qal of שאל (ask) with tone retracted in
pause with *athnach* and original vowel appearing,
DG 40, WL 117, GK 29*m*.

לָעוֹז, prep. *lamedh* with *qamets* in pretone (as above),
plus inf. cstr. qal of עזז (be strong). So EVV and
Versions generally. Kittel reads לעוז from the root
עוז (take refuge), and the parallelism seems to demand
this root, but the form of MT is impossible for an
ayin-vav (*u*) verb. Possibly the *o*-vowel, though
anomalous, is intentional in order to secure an
assonance; cf. GK 72*q*. See the following note.

מעוז, prep. *beth* plus sing. cstr. of מָעוֹז (strength)
from the root עזז. MT treats all the forms of מעוז,
whether with or without suffixes, as if from the double-
ayin root, whereas it is certain that in some cases the
meaning 'refuge' is intended, as if from the *ayin-vav*
root, GK 85*k*, BDB 731*b*. Cheyne would point מְעוֹז,
as true cstr. sing. of מָעוֹז (refuge, stronghold, from

42

עוּז), which some read (see RVm), taking the previous verb to be from the *ayin-vav* root, as Kittel.

לַחְסוֹת, prep. *lamedh* plus inf. cstr. qal of חסה (take refuge). The firmly closed syllable occurs after *lamedh* in four forms, GK 63*i*.

Verse 3. פַרְעֹה. Duhm, Cheyne, Box treat this and the following בְּצֵל מִצְרַיִם as unrhythmical glosses. It is possible that the first may be, though unlikely, but there is little likelihood of the second being a gloss.

הֶחָסוּת, article plus חָסוּת (refuge), a noun found only here in OT.

Verse 4. שָׂרָיו, 'his princes', Box says 'of Judah', but most say 'of Pharaoh'. The *qamets* under the *sin* is firm, the root being double-*ayin*.

חַנֵם יַגִּיעוּ, 'arrive at (or 'reach to', Skinner) Hanes'. Zoan, at the N.E. extremity of the delta, and Hanes S. of Memphis mark the northern and southern limits of Lower Egypt. Cheyne reads תַּחְפַּנֵס, Tahpanhes, which receives some support from T. LXX has μάτην κοπιάσουσιν (labour in vain), reading חִנָּם יִגָּעוּ. The fact that eighteen Heb. MSS. have חנם does not indicate a variant MT reading, but shows assimilation to LXX.

Verse 5. הֵבִישׁ. The Qere is הֹבִישׁ, 3 m. s. pf. hiph. of בּוֹשׁ (be ashamed), but as if from the root יבשׁ, DG 152, GK 78*b*. So Jewish tradition and the Versions, except LXX which does not express the phrase at all. The Kethib is הִבְאִישׁ, 3 m. s. pf. hiph. of באשׁ (stink). Krochmal, Cheyne, Kittel, Graetz, and Box dislike both readings and prefer כֻּלָּם הֵבִיאוּ שַׁי (they have all of them brought gifts). Procksch suggests כֹּל הַבָּא הֹבִישׁ (everyone that cometh shall be ashamed).

43

לא יועילו, relative clause without conjunction, DS 191, GK 155*f*. The root יעל is found only in the hiphil.

למו, prep. *lamedh* plus 3 m. p. personal suffix, 'poetic' form occurring fifty-three times, GK 103*f* (note 3, p. 302). Duhm, Cheyne, Kittel read לְעָם and begin the second half of the verse with it, 'to a people which is no help', and then omit ולא הועיל, which is not in LXX, as a variant of the similar phrase earlier in the verse. This suggestion has a great deal to recommend it.

כי is here an adversative, though usually we find כי אם after a negative, DS 203, GK 163*a*.

Verse 6. משׂא. There are two words, one meaning 'load, burden', and the other (as here) meaning 'oracle', i.e. that which the prophet says when he lifts up his voice.

בהמות, cstr. pl. of בְּהֵמָה (beast). Skinner and Kittel prefer בְּשִׁמּוֹת, 'in the wastes of the Negeb'. It is better, in our view, to follow LXX with בְּהֵמוֹת, i.e. 'The Oracle concerning the Behemoth of the Negeb', being a reference to Egypt as the Rahab of the old Creation myth. See verse 7 (note).

לביא and ליש are two of the half-dozen words for 'lion'. It is said that Arabic has thirty words.

מהם, prep. *min* plus 3 m. p. suffix. Klosterman, and most moderns, read נֹהֵם, 'growling' of a lion devouring his prey, as against שׁאג which is his roar when he springs; cf. v. 29; also BDB 625*a*. Good.

אפעה is a kind of viper. A noun with *aleph* as preformative, here 'essential' and not 'euphonic'; cf. Arabic 'elative', GK 85*b*.

שׂרף, a venomous serpent with a *burning* bite. Probably distinct from the Seraphim, who are personifications of the lightnings. Cf. articles in HDB (Strachan) and EB (Cheyne).

מְעוֹפֵף, m. ptc. poel of עוּף (fly). Only here and xiv. 29, and each time of 'flying fiery serpent', probably a fabulous Egyptian snake monster with wings; see article 'Serpent' in HDB.

יִשְׂאוּ, 3 m. p. impf. qal of נָשָׂא (lift up, carry), with the *nun-dagesh* failing over the vocal *sheva*, DG 33, WL 20, GK 20*m*.

עֲיָרִים, both Kethib and Qere, so Norzi and Kahle, following both the Leningrad and Cairo MSS. Many Bibles have עוּרִים Kethib and עִירִים Qere. Plural of עַיִר (male ass).

חֵילֵיהֶם, pl. of חַיִל (here 'wealth') plus 3 m. p. suff., being parallel to 'their treasures'. Kahle omits the second *yod*, but Norzi and all other authorities, except the Leningrad and Cairo MSS., write *yod* twice.

דַּבֶּשֶׁת, only here of the hump of the camel, so BDB and the American Jewish translation (1916). The EVV. follow the early Versions, though LXX omits. The etymology is unknown. The word occurs in Joshua xix. 11 as a place-name.

גְּמַלִּים. The *lamedh* is doubled, according to GK 93*s*, *ee*, to keep the preceding vowel short. Since, however, the doubled radical in all such cases is usually a weak liquid, it is probably doubled to ensure its proper pronunciation, so that the short vowel is a secondary matter, and is due to Masoretic principles concerning the pretone vowel.

Verse 7. וּמִצְרַיִם. Most moderns regard this as a gloss on the preceding phrase, probably correctly. The correct Masoretic translation is 'and as for Egypt', i.e. a *casus pendens*, marked by the accent *zaqeph-gadhol*.

D   45

Haupt, treating as gloss, translated 'that is, Egypt'.

יעזרו, 3 m. p. imf. qal of עזר (help) with tone retracted and original *o*-vowel reappearing. The *sheva* is usually closed with this root, GK 63*c*.

רהב, Rahab, the mythical dragon of the Creation Myth, here identified, as regularly in the Bible, with the Oppressor of Israel and the Enemy of God. See Gunkel, *Schöpfung und Chaos* (2nd ed., 1921), and Snaith, *Studies in the Psalter* (1934), pp. 94–109.

הם שבת. Read הַמָּשְׁבָּת, 'therefore have I called her, Rahab that is stilled'. Some prefer, though inadequately, הַמִּשְׁבִּית 'that stilleth'. The Masoretic Text is 'Rahab are they: inaction', the correct accents being *merkha, tiphkha*. Wickes quotes four MSS. which have the accents *tiphkha, merkha*, in which case the translation is 'Rahab: they are inaction'. Various other suggestions have been made, e.g. Duhm הַמָּשִׁמֹּת (Rahab the great chaos), the plural being a plural of majesty, DS 18, GK 124*g–i*; Procksch, רָהְבָּה מָשְׁבָּת (her pride is stilled); Houbigant, הֶרְפָּה וּבֹשֶׁת (. . . is a reproach and a shame).

Verse 8. עתה. Some MSS. have ועתה, but this is assimilating to LXX.

בוא, 2 m. s. imperat. qal of בּוֹא (come).

כתבה, 2 m. s. imperat. qal of כתב (write) plus 3 f. s. suffix (for neuter), DS 17 (Rem. 2), GK 122*q* (and note). Pronounce *koth-e-vah*, with a short-*o*.

אתם. Presumably 'in their presence', but this use of the prep. אֵת is rare, BDB 86*a* (1*c*). Duhm, Cheyne, Box and Procksch omit.

חקה, 2 m. s. imperat. qal of חקק (inscribe) plus 3 f. s. suffix.

ותהי, weak-*vav* plus 3 f. s. (for neuter, but see GK

46

135p) jussive qal, 'that it may be', DS 199, DT chap. v, GK 109*f*.

לָעֵד, 'for ever', but read with T, S and V, and moderns לְעֵד 'for a witness'. MT has been influenced by the following word in favour of a familiar phrase.

Verse 9. עַם מְרִי, lit. 'a people of rebellion', the latter word being a noun, DS 32, GK 128*t*.

כְּחָשִׁים, m. p. of. adj. כֶּחָשׁ (lying). The *cheth* is virtually doubled, so that the *seghol* is firm, GK 84*e*.

לֹא אָבִי וג׳, relative clause without the relative conjunction, DS 191, GK 155*f*.

Verse 10. לֹא תִרְאוּ, 'thou shalt not see', a strong prohibition, being לֹא with the imperfect. אַל with the jussive means 'don't', DG 83, WL 77, DS 86, DT 54 (obs.), GK 109*c*, 152*b*.

לָנוּ, prep. *lamedh* with 1 pl. suffix, expressing 'ethical dative', 'with regard to us', WL 207 (top), DS 140, GK 143*e*.

נְכֹחוֹת, f. pl. of adj. נָכֹחַ (straight). The fem. pl. is used as a substantive in place of the Latin and Greek neuter, DS 16, GK 122*q*.

מַהֲתַלּוֹת (deceits). The root is presumably תלל, but BDB does not give the word either under this or under the root התל, with which there is confusion; cf. BDB pp. 251, 1068.

Verse 11. מִנִּי. The form occurs twice only for the normal *min*, and both in this verse. Probably a poetic by-form on the analogy of עֲדֵי and עֲלֵי, GK 102*b*.

הַטּוּ, 2 m. p. imperat. hiph. of נטה (turn aside).

Verse 12. מָאָסְכֶם, inf. cstr. qal of מאס (reject) plus 2 m. p. suffix. Pronounce *mo-os-e-kem*, with short-*o* twice. The *metheg* with *qamets* does not always indicate a long-*a*.

47

וּתְבִטְחוּ, strong-*vav* plus 2 m. p. impf. qal of בטח (trust), following inf. cstr., both having a sense equivalent to the perfect, DS 74.

בְּעֹשֶׁק, 'in oppression', but most scholars read בְּעָקֵשׁ, 'in a perverted one', with support from the 'lie' of the Targum שְׁקָרָא and of the LXX ψεύδει. See also the parallel word נלוז. Kittel and Box make בעקש a gloss on the following word, for which they read בנלוז.

נלוז, niph. ptc. of לוז, and so 'crooked, turned aside'. LXX read the root לון (ἐγόγγυσας, 'and because thou didst murmur').

וּתִשָּׁעֵנוּ, strong-*vav* plus 2 m. p. impf. niph. of שען, 'and ye have supported yourselves on him', i.e. on the perverted and crooked one.

Verse 13. עון means both 'iniquity' and 'punishment' as a result of it; cf. Genesis iv. 13. It is a 'sword of Damocles'.

נפל, act. ptc. qal used as *fut. instans* 'ready (or "about") to fall', DS 134, GK 116*d*, *e*.

נבעה, m. s. ptc. niph. of בעה. The root means both 'seek' and 'swell', the original probably being of 'swelling out, up', and so metaphorically of 'earnest desire, ardent seeking'. Here either 'swelling, enlarging' of a crack (Dillmann), or better 'swelling out' of a decaying wall. Kittel thinks the word is a gloss.

בחומה. T and S have the prep. *kaph*.

נשגבה, f. s. ptc. niph. of שגב (be inaccessibly high).

Verse 14. וּשְׁבָרָהּ, strong-*vav* plus 3 m. s. pf. qal plus 3 f. s. suffix, 'and he shall break it', but Kittel and Procksch think, probably correctly, that it is a dittograph of the previous word.

יצרום. Note the plural; not 'like a potter's vessel', but 'like a potters' vessel'.

48

כתות, pass. ptc. qal, 'crushed fine'. Van der Hoogt's edition has כָּתוֹת (inf. abs.), which makes better sense, and is suggested by Kittel, but the ptc. is certainly the true MT.

ולא־ימצא, 'so that there cannot be found'. The weak-*vav* with the imperfect equals the Greek ἵνα, DS 90, GK 120c. The imperfect can be used for all kinds of auxiliary verbs, DS 64, DT 43, GK 107k, and here equals 'can'.

לחתות, prep. *lamedh* plus inf. cstr. qal of חתה ('snatch up', usually of fire).

לחשׂף, prep. *lamedh* plus inf. cstr. qal of חשׂף, properly 'strip off', and so 'skim' of water and wine. LXX has ἀποσυριεῖς, which presumably is from ἀποσυρίζω (whistle aloud, hiss), but it is probably an error for ἀποσύρεις, from ἀποσύρω (tear away, strip), which indeed a small number of cursives read.

גבא is a place where water collects. The word is rare in OT, found only here and Ezekiel xlvii. 11, where it apparently means 'marshes'. Translate here 'cistern' or 'pond', as in Rabbinic Hebrew. LXX could make nothing of the word in either case.

Verse 15. בשׁובה, prep. *beth* plus noun שׁוּבָה, not found elsewhere. It is from the root שׁוב, and is generally interpreted either as turning away from the Egyptian policy, or as averseness to war; cf. Micah ii. 8. It is best to interpret as 'turning back', i.e. repentance; cf. the name Shear-yashub, which means 'a remnant shall repent'. Ehrlich, Cheyne, and Box suggest בְּשֶׁבֶת (in sitting still), being prep. *beth* plus inf. cstr. qal of ישׁב (sit). Retain MT.

ונחת, copula *vav* (with *qamets* in pretone, DG 53, WL 45) plus נחַת noun from the root נוח, meaning

49

'quietness, rest'. Ehrlich's suggestion in the previous verse brings the word there closer to the meaning here, but the Versions have taken this word to mean 'repent', thus assimilating to the meaning of MT in the previous word. Presumably they read נִחַם. Cf. Hosea xiii. 14.

תּוֹשֵׁעוּן, 2 m. p. impf. niph. of ישׁע (save) with final emphatic *nun*, carrying the tone and setting up a secondary tone with the accent *munach* under *vav*, GK 47*m*.

בְּהַשְׁקֵט, prep. *beth* plus inf. abs. hiph. of שׁקט (be quiet), used as a substantive, GK 113*h*. LXX varies considerably.

Verse 16. לֹא־כִי. The *maqqeph* is difficult. Either omit it, or follow the suggestion of Syr. and read לֹא־כֵן, 'Not so'. If the *maqqeph* is omitted and the כי transferred to the next phrase, it can be either the adversative (GK 163*a*, though it should properly be כִּי אִם), or a particle introducing direct narrative (GK 157*b*). LXX omits both words.

נָנוּס. Skinner suggests that here this verb should be translated 'we will fly (against the enemy)', but it is better to think of the flight to Egypt for help.

תְּנוּסוּן, 2 m. p. impf. qal of נוּס (flee), with final emphatic *nun*, taking the tone, GK 47*m*.

נִרְכָּב, 1 pl. impf. qal of רכב (ride). The normal vowel is *pathach*, and the *qamets* here is in pause with *zaqeph qaton*.

יִקַּלּוּ, 3 m. p. impf. niph. of קלל, stative double-*ayin* verb; 'shall show themselves swift'.

Verse 17. אֶלֶף אֶחָד is not good Hebrew, as Cheyne pointed out. A verb is necessary, as LXX has seen with its φεύξονται, which the English Versions have followed with their 'shall flee'. Either substitute for

אחד (or insert) a verb which means 'shall flee', or omit the phrase as a gloss, as Duhm, Cheyne, Procksch, Box. Suggested verbs are יָנוּסוּ, 'shall flee' (LXX, Kissane), יֵחַתּוּ, 'shall be terrified' (Graetz), יֶחֱרַד, 'shall tremble' (Kittel). Kissane goes farther and at the end of 17a would insert רִבּוֹ, 'a myriad (shall flee)', on the basis of the LXX πολλοί (many) for רַבִּים. This is an excellent suggestion.

עַד אִם. The אִם follows עַד pleonastically here and thrice elsewhere, whilst עַד אֲשֶׁר אִם occurs thrice. The prep. עַד tends to need strengthening in later style, DS 141.

נוֹתַרְתֶּם, 2 m. p. pf. niph. of יתר (remain over), here equivalent to the classical future perfect.

תרן. Derivation unknown, but see Ezekiel xxvii. 5. The 'beacon' of the English Versions is from the Targum בּוֹעֲרָא (torch, fire-signal), but the other Versions have 'mast', whilst V leaves no doubt with its *malus navis* (mast of a ship).

Verse 18. יְחַכֶּה, 3 m. s. impf. piel of חכה (await). The root occurs once only in the qal, and this at the end of this verse as m. pl. cstr. of act. ptc. followed by prep. *lamedh*, a frequent variation from the strict construct use, DS 37, GK 130a.

לְחָנְנְכֶם, prep. *lamedh* plus חָנַן, inf. cstr. qal of חנן I (be compassionate to) plus 2 m. p. suff. The normal double-*ayin* form would be חֹן, but the forms חֲנָנָה and חֲנָנְכֶם are found with suffixes, and חַנּוֹת without suffix, GK 67ee, BDB 335f. The existence of the double-*nun* has given rise to many curious variations.

יָרוּם, 3 m. s. impf. qal of רום (be high, exalted). So the Versions, and probably even Targum with תַּקִּיף

(strong, mighty) since this word stands for גבה (high) in Isaiah x. 33. Most scholars read יִדֹּם, 3 m. s. impf. qal of דמם (be silent), which a few Hebrew MSS. read. This accords well with the previous 'wait'.

לרחמכם, prep. *lamedh* plus inf. cstr. piel of רחם (in piel 'to have compassion') plus 2 m. pl. suff. Note the *seghol* which comes in to avoid two vocal *shevas* after the manner of the third declension. The *cheth* is virtually doubled, as usual in *ayin-cheth* verbs.

אשרי, cstr. pl. of אֶשֶׁר (or אֹשֶׁר), a noun meaning 'blessedness, happiness'. The plural is intensive, DS 18 (§ 16c), GK 124a; 'O the great happiness of . . .'. Cf. xxxii. 20.

Verse 19. . . . כִּי־עַם. MT reads, 'For a people in Zion shall dwell in Jerusalem'. LXX has, 'For a holy people shall dwell in Zion' and takes 'Jerusalem' with the next clause, omitting the negative two words later. So Syr., but retaining the negative. V has, 'For the people of Zion shall dwell in Jerusalem'. All the Versions found the line difficult. Most moderns read יֹשֵׁב (the act. ptc. qal), and translate, 'For, O people that dwelleth in Zion in Jerusalem'. An attractive suggestion is by Procksch, who would insert עַם יהוה after 'Jerusalem', and translate, 'For a people shall dwell in Zion, the people of the Lord in Jerusalem'. Kissane treats 'in Jerusalem' as a gloss.

בכו, inf. abs. qal of בכה (weep). This form is found five times against the normal *lamedh-he* form with final *he* (four times). The variation is frequent, GK 75n. The inf. abs. strengthens the denial, and the negative properly comes in between the two verbal forms, DS 118, GK 113o. In Genesis iii. 4 the whole statement of Elohim is being denied.

52

יְחָנְךָ, 3 m. s. impf. qal of חנן (be gracious to) plus 2 m. s. suff. Pronounce *yoch-ne-kha* with short-*o*. The form יְחָנְךָ is found in Genesis xliii. 29. The normal impf. qal is יָחֹן, with a tendency for the first vowel to become short-*o* instead of short-*a* with suffixes. The verb has many unusual forms, due to its being a *pe*-guttural verb as well as a double-*ayin* verb with doubled-*nun*, a weak consonant. See GK 67*n*, and BDB *in loc*.

זַעֲקֶךָ, inf. cstr. qal זְעֹק (GK 54*c*) plus 2 m. s. suff. (normally זַעֲקְךָ) with tone retracted in pause with *zaqeph qaton*. Baer reads *sheva* under the *ayin*, but *chateph-pathach* is the sounder reading.

כְּשָׁמְעָתוֹ, prep. *kaph* plus שָׁמְעָה (*shom-'ah* with short-*o*), a fem. form of inf. cstr. qal (GK 45*d*) of שמע (hear) plus 3 m. s. suff. Translate 'when he hears' or, better, 'as soon as he heareth', DT 21.

עָנָךְ, 3 m. s. p. qal of ענה I (answer) plus the suffix -*akh*, which is found once as 2 f. s. suff. in Isaiah lx. 9 and four times as 2 m. s. suffix in pause, as here, GK 58*g*. The perfect is unexpected here, but is explained as the 'perfect of confidence', DS 61, or as the prophetic perfect, DT 121.

Verse 20. ונתן, strong-*vav* plus perfect, 'and though the Lord give thee . . .', so Cheyne.

לחם is in the absolute, as also the following מים, the two phrases being cases of apposition where the second member limits and qualifies the first, DS 40, GK 131*b*.

צר. Noun meaning 'distress'. Many MSS. and editions have *pathach*, but *qamets* is the sounder text. This is what the Targum read, and so Kahle, following both the Cairo and the Leningrad MSS., and so also the accurate Brit. Mus. MS. Or. 2627.

מוֹרֶיךָ. Noun מוֹרֶה (the form is hiph. ptc. of יָרָה),
meaning 'teacher'. According to AV, the noun is in
the plural with 2 m. s. suffix, meaning the true prophets
who have been driven into concealment, but both
LXX and Syriac understood it of the prophets who
had led the people astray. On the other hand, the
Targum understands the noun to be in the singular
and to refer to God Himself, and so also the Vulgate.
This is the reading of RVm, and most moderns after
Ewald and Wellhausen, though Delitzsch, Cheyne and
Kittel disagree. If the noun is regarded as a plural,
then the verb יִכָּנֵף is 3 m. s. impf. niph. (used im-
personally as a passive, DS 112, GK 121*b*) with the
noun as an accusative. In this case the verb, only
here and a denominative from כָּנָף (wing, extremity),
is used in the original sense of the root as 'driven into
a corner', and not by way of the metaphor of 'hidden
under a wing'. If, on the other hand, the noun is
regarded as a singular, then it is the subject of the
sentence, and the sense is the derived one of 'hiding'.
For the retention of the *yodh* with suffixes in the
singular of *lamedh-he* nouns, see GK 93*ss*.

רָאוֹת, f. pl. of act. ptc. qal of רָאָה (see). All predicates
of dual nouns are plurals, DS 157, GK 145*n*.

Verse 21. מֵאַחֲרֶיךָ, 'a word from behind thee'.
Kittel, who holds to the 'teachers' in the previous
verse, would here read דְּבַר מְאַשְּׁרֶיךָ, 'the word of those
that bless thee', but Kissane's suggestion is much more
attractive, מְאָרְחֶיךָ, 'the word of thy Guide', i.e. m. p.
ptc. piel of a denominative of the noun אֹרַח (path)
plus 2 m. s. (*sic*) suffix. The verb is used in Ethiopic,
with the meaning 'conduct, guide'.

תַּאֲמִינוּ, 2 m. p. imf. hiph. of אָמַן (believe), but it is evident that the root ימן is intended, a denominative of the noun יָמִין (right hand). Read therefore more accurately תֵּימִינוּ. So all Versions and moderns.

תשמאילו, 2 m. p. impf. hiph. of the quadrilateral root שׂמאל, a denominative 'turn to the left', GK 56.

Verse 22. וטמאתם strong-*vav* plus 2 m. p. pf. piel of טמא (defile). LXX, OL, and V (but not T and S) have the singular, which most moderns would read here (cf. the verbs in the second half of the verse), but such a change of person as MT shows is common, and there is no need to alter the text, GK 145*m*. In LXX, Cod. A and the correctors of א have ἐξαρεῖς (and he shall carry away). This is due either to second half of the verse, or to reading וַהֲמַסֹּתָם hiph. of מוֹשׁ (cause to be moved, overthrown). This reading makes better sense, and refers to the removal of the valuable coverings of the idols, preparatory to the destruction of the less valuable material.

צִפּוּי, cstr. sing. of noun (plating), being a passive form from צפה II (overlay). Tr. 'the silver plating of thy idols', and, in the next phrase, 'the golden sheathing of your images', GK 135*n*. Note the survival of the original *lamedh-yodh*, as in the pass. ptc. qal forms of *lamedh-he* verbs, GK 84*ᵃc* (ε).

פסילי, cstr. pl. of פָּסִיל, properly a hewn idol, though it is frequently used of a metal (cast) image.

אפדת, cstr. sing. of the fem. form אֲפֻדָּה, which supplies the cstr. and suffix forms for the masc. form אֵפֹד. The translation, 'sheathing, covering', depends upon an original meaning of the ephod as that which covers the image (whence 'ephod' to mean the image itself) or the priest (whence the 'linen ephod' to mean the slight garment of the priest of pre-exilic times. See BDB 65.

מסכה, cstr. sing. of מַסֵּכָה (that which is poured out), from the root נסך I, whence the noun can mean either 'libation' or 'molten image'.

תזרם, 2 m. s. impf. qal of זרה (scatter) plus 3 m. p. suffix. Translate 'thou shalt scatter them'. LXX has a double translation, due to the use of the root in connection with threshing, 'thou shalt make them small and shalt scatter them away'. Kittel suggests תְּזִרֵם, 'thou shalt make them loathsome', thus forming a parallel to the opening verb of the verse, and parsing as an impf. hiph. with 3 m. p. suffix from זוּר I (make estranged, loathsome), unless there really is a second root, 'to be loathsome', BDB 266.

דוה, f. s. of adj. דָּוֶה (faint, unwell), here 'a menstruous thing'. Delitzsch would understand כְּלִי (vessel), but this is not necessary.

צא, 2 m. s. imperat. qal of יצא (go out). Kittel suggests צֹאָה (filth, excrement), which may originally have been intended.

תאמר, 2 m. s. impf. qal with tone retracted because of the accented syllable which follows, GK 29*e*. The *maqqeph* which Baer inserts in his text is without justification.

Verse 23. מטר זרעך, lit. 'the rain of thy seed', i.e. 'thy seed-rain'—namely, the 'early-rain', the October monsoon rains.

ירעה, 3 m. s. impf. qal of רעה (pasture), but it is better to read וְרָעָה, strong-*vav* plus pf., 'and (thy cattle) shall feed . . .', as Versions and moderns.

מקניך, 2 m. s. suffix to the singular מִקְנֶה. The

56

apparently plural suffix is due to the original *yodh* of the *lamedh-he* (-*yodh*) root, GK 93*ss*. Some forty-five MSS. omit the *yodh*, but the true text has it.

כֵּר, 'pasture'. The derivation is uncertain, whether from כַּר (lamb) or from the root כרר and so 'round enclosure'.

Verse 24. עבדי האדמה, 'who work the land'.

בליל. If this word is from בלל I, then the meaning is 'mixed' fodder, but there is an Arabic word *bullat*, which means 'the moisture of fresh pasture'; cf. the Syriac meaning, 'fresh corn'. The former is more likely to be correct, because of the following word which means 'seasoned', i.e. to make it more tasty; cf. RVm, 'salted', but the root has rather to do with bitter vinegar. V has *commistum migma*, i.e. 'mixed mixture', which Douai renders as 'bran'.

יאכלו, 3 m. p. impf. qal of אכל (eat). The tone is retracted in pause with *athnach*, and the *tsere* appears in the plural form, as always, instead of the expected *pathach*, GK 68*e*.

זרה, act. ptc. qal of זרה, 'which (one) winnows'. Kittel and others would read either זֹרָה (pual pf.) or זָרָה (qal pf.), but the change is not necessary.

רחת. Found only here in OT, apparently meaning 'winnowing shovel' as distinct from מִזְרֶה, which is the six-pronged winnowing fork. T and S support MT, but LXX and V have 'winnowed with barley' and 'winnowed in the floor' respectively.

Verse 25. נשאה, f. s. of niph. ptc. of נשׂא (lift up).

פלגים, properly 'channels'; cf. Assyrian *palgu* (irrigation channel), though it is not necessary to assume that it must be an artificial canal.

יבלי, cstr. p. of (probably) יָבָל (watercourse, con-

57

duit) from the root יבל (bear along). The phrase is in apposition to the previous word.

הרג רב, '(in a day of) great slaughter', so the English Versions, following T and S, but LXX and V think of 'the slaughter of many', reading either רַבִּים or רֹב.

Verse 26. שבעתים, multiplication is expressed by the dual of the fem. numeral, DG 165, WL 197*f*, DS 56, GK 134*r*. The three following words are an obvious gloss, and are not in LXX.

מכתו, 3 m. s. suff. to the sing. מַכָּה (stroke). The root is *pe-nun*, hence the *dagesh*.

Verse 27. בא is the act. ptc. qal after הנה.

. . . בער, lit. 'burning is his anger, and heaviness is the uplifted (cloud)'.

משאה. T has 'and too heavy to be borne', i.e. וְכָבֵד מַנְּשָׂא. V is similar with *gravis ad portandum* (Douai 'is heavy to bear'). Kittel, Kissane suggest וְכָבֵד מַשָּׂאָה, 'and heavy is his load', and so (nearly) Procksch, with וְכָבֵד, which is better still.

Verse 28. רוחו, 'and his strong breath', since the word רוח carries the idea of irresistible power.

יחצה, 3 m. s. impf. qal of חצה (halve), i.e. 'it shall reach up to the neck and divide men in half' according to the interpretation of the Targum. S has 'and shall cut off the neck', V 'to the middle of the neck', LXX 'shall come up to the neck, and be divided'. It seems that all read much the same text, and found it difficult.

להנפה, prep. *lamedh* plus inf. cstr. hiph. of נוף (wave to and fro), either 'sift as in a sieve' (EVV) or 'winnow with a fan' (Dillmann, Duhm, Cheyne). The hiph. inf.

cstr. is normally הָנִיף, but here we have an added feminine ending, GK 72z, but it may be due to the normal inf. haphel of Biblical and Palestinian Aramaic. The Versions, however, do not seem to have recognized the metaphor of the sieve, but speak of 'confusing' them (LXX) or of 'destroying' them (V), but since both T and S have 'exciting, agitating', it is probable that neither the LXX or V represent a text substantially different.

נפת, cstr. s. of נָפָה, with a firm *qamets* due to the *ayin-vav* root. Probably a 'sieve' or some winnowing instrument. The word is used in the Talmud (*b. Chull.* 45a) of something that is perforated, so presumably 'sieve' is the true meaning. LXX and V have no corresponding word.

Verse 29. התקדש, inf. cstr. hithp. of קדש (be holy), with *seghol* for *tsere* before *maqqeph*, 'when one hallows the Feast', i.e. as at the opening of the great Autumnal Harvest Feast which marked the end of one year and the beginning of the next. The reference is to the all-night celebrations of the first night.

Verse 30. נחת (descent), cstr. sing. of noun from נחת (go down, descend), a regular Aramaic root, used occasionally in Hebrew, chiefly in poetry. There is another noun of the same form from נוח (rest).

יראה, 3 m. s. impf. hiph. of ראה (see).

Verse 31. יחת, 3 m. s. impf. qal of חתת (be shattered, dismayed). Imperfects of double-*ayin* roots in -a have *tsere* in the first syllable, GK 67n.

יכה, 3 m. s. impf. hiph. of נכה (smite), but Duhm, Kittel and most moderns would point as the hoph. יֻכֶּה, though all are inclined to regard the word as a gloss, thus restoring the metre.

Verse 32. The whole verse is difficult and 'full of hopeless obscurities' (Skinner). Translate 'And it shall be, every passing over of the rod of foundation (read with most מוּסָרָה, "correction" or better, with Duhm and others, מוּסָרֹה, "his corrective rod"), which the Lord shall cause to rest upon him (that it shall be) with tabrets and harps (for us), but with battles of shaking will he fight with them'. The Versions vary, but give little help.

אֲשֶׁר יָנִיחַ יְהוָֹה עָלָיו is probably a gloss, so most moderns.

וּבְמִלְחָמוֹת. The suggested וּבִמְחֹלֹת, i.e. 'and in shaking dances', does not appear to improve the sense.

בה. The Kethib is בָּהּ 'with her', i.e. Jerusalem (LXX and S), and the Qere בָּם 'with them', i.e. with the enemy (V and T).

Verse 33. מֵאֶתְמוּל. There are two words which are distinct. Firstly, מוּל (root מוּל) with *shureq* is a substantive used as a preposition to mean 'in front of'. Secondly, אֶתְמוֹל (root תמל) with *cholem* is a substantive used as an adverb to mean 'yesterday, recently'. The former is found twice anomalously with *cholem*, Deuteronomy i. 1 and (with *aleph* also) Nehemiah xii. 38. The latter is found, as here, twice anomalously with *shureq*. The other instance is Micah ii. 8. The passage in Micah is almost certainly corrupt, and most moderns would read *cholem* here. The Versions have all translated as if the *cholem* were written, though Targum has a conflate rendering which includes both.

תָּפְתֶּה. Either a variant form of the masc. תֹּפֶת

60

(Olshausen) or it should be תָּפְתֹּה, 'his Topheth' (Stade). The former is more likely. The original was probably תֹּפֶת or תֹּפֶת, but it was pointed by the Masoretes with the vowels of בֹּשֶׁת (shame) because of the idolatrous associations.

גַּם־הוּא לַמֶּלֶךְ is generally considered a gloss, though it is represented in all the Versions. It is probably a note to say that Topheth is associated with the Molech-worship, 2 Kings xxiii. 10. The Qere is הִיא, GK 32*l*.

הוּכַן, 3 m. s. pf. hoph. of כּוּן (there hath been prepared), DS 154, GK 121*a*. Some editions have *pathach*, which is the normal vowel, but *qamets* is undoubtedly the sounder tradition, so Qimchi and Norzi.

הֶעְמִיק, 3 m. s. pf. hiph. of עמק (stative verb in -*o*, 'to be deep'). The hiphil is transitive, DS 108, 'he hath made it deep'. Duhm and many moderns would read the inf. abs. הַעֲמִיק, and similarly for the following הַרְחֵב. This would be idiomatic, but the change is not essential.

מְדֻרָתָה, 'as for its pile', i.e. funeral pyre. This is a *casus pendens*, marked, as often, by the accent *rebhia*.

אֵשׁ. Either substitute קַשׁ (stubble) with Duhm, or, with Skinner and others, insert גַּחֲלֵי to read 'coals of fire'.

עֵצִים. The plural denotes 'logs', as separate portions taken from the whole, GK 124*l*. Hence the LXX use of ξύλον (a cut log) for even the singular of עֵץ. It is used even for a live tree, a use which is rare outside Alexandrian Greek. This is the origin of the NT use of ξύλον for the Cross.

הַרְבֵּה. This inf. abs. hiph. of רבה is used as an adverb to mean 'exceedingly, greatly'.

נשמה, cstr. sing. of נְשָׁמָה, which is properly ordinary smooth breathing as against רוּחַ, which is strong, emphatic breathing.

בערה, fem. sing. of act. qal ptc. of בער (burn). The idea is of burning out, as is shown by the Syriac meaning, 'seek out, collect, glean'.

CHAPTER XXXI

Verse 1. על. Some editions have ועל, including Jacob ben Chaim, but the majority of the best authorities omit the *vav*, as do all the ancient Versions except the Targum.

סוּם is properly the chariot horse, especially when the reference is to Egypt. The cavalry horse is פָּרָשׁ.

יִשְׁעֵנוּ, 3 m. p. impf. niph. of שׁען, 'they support themselves', with tone retracted in pause and original *tsere* reappearing. Duhm would read יִשְׁעוּ from the root שׁעה, translating 'they look (for help)'; cf. 2 Samuel xxii. 42. The suggestion is made on the basis of the LXX πεποιθότες, 'who rely on', which does provide a parallel for the next word. Keep MT. It is unlikely that the writer would use the word here as a parallel for 'trust', and later in the same verse as a parallel for 'inquire, seek'.

רכב is a collective noun, meaning 'chariotry', and rarely 'a chariot', which is מֶרְכָּבָה.

פָּרָשִׁים, 'horsemen'. The *qamets* under the *pe* is firm, as a compensation for a doubled *resh*, GK 93*dd*. The Hebrew for 'horses' is פָּרָשִׁים.

Verse 2. וְגַם־הוּא. Note the emphatic and ironical
'and yet He too is wise'.

וַיָּבֵא, strong-*vav* plus 3 m. s. impf. hiph. (jussive form
according to rule) of בּוֹא, 'and hath brought', and so
the Versions. The English Versions have 'and will
bring', which represents a Hebrew וְיָבִיא, and is better,
especially in view of the later strong-*vav* with perfect
וְקָם, 'and will arise'.

Verse 3. יִכְלָיוּן, 3 m. p. imf. qal of כלה (be at an
end) with the original *lamedh-yodh* reappearing in
pause before the full archaic and emphatic ending
in -*un*, GK 75*u*.

Verse 4. יֶהְגֶּה. The root הגה I is properly 'to make
a low murmuring sound', and hence 'soliloquize'
(Psalm i. 4), 'coo' of a dove (Isaiah xxxviii. 14), 'sigh
for' as in mourning (Isaiah xvi. 7), and 'growl' as
a lion over its prey, as here. It is a low, inarticulate
sound.

. . . אֲשֶׁר יִקָּרֵא, 'against whom there has been rallied
a full muster of shepherds'.

יֵחָת, 3 m. s. impf. qal of חתת (be dismayed, terrified),
with *qamets* for *pathach* under *zaqeph-qaton* in pause.
The imperfect is of 'general custom', DS 66, DT 37*f*,
GK 107*f*.

יַעֲנֶה, 3 m. s. impf. qal of ענה III (be bowed down,
afflicted), 'and because of their thronging (bustle) he
is not disturbed (put out)'. Targum and Syriac have
the niphal, which is possibly better. The simile is of
the lion being undisturbed in spite of all the tumult
and shouting of a crowd of men whom he despises
because of their weakness and inability. This view is
demanded because of verse 5, where it is clear that
Jehovah's descent is to protect Jerusalem and not to
join in the fight against her. Jerusalem's business is

to rest quiet and unresisting in Jehovah's power, and
Jehovah like the lion will be quite unperturbed by
all the shouting of those who are trying to get
Jerusalem out of His clutches. The prep. עַל should
therefore be translated 'upon' and not 'against'.

Verse 5. צִפֹּר is a third declension noun in which the
-*o* of the final syllable has not entirely disappeared
with the suffix.

עָפוֹת, f. pl. of act. ptc. qal of עוּף (fly).

יָגֵן, 3 m. s. impf. hiph. of גנן (cover, defend),
though Barth holds that it is the impf. qal, instancing
an Arabic form with final -*i*.

וְהִצִּיל, strong-*vav* plus 3 m. s. pf. hiph., and similarly
for the following וְהִמְלִיט. Translate '(covering) and he
will deliver, passing over and he will preserve'. But
we would naturally expect all four forms to be inf.
absolutes instead of two only, GK 113*t*. Read therefore, with most moderns, וְהַצֵּיל and וְהַמְלֵיט.

Verse 6. The verse is really untranslatable, since
even if we insert (or assume the strong ellipsis of)
מִמֶּנּוּ, 'from him', לַאֲשֶׁר cannot strictly be rendered 'to
whom', since אֲשֶׁר is a relative and not a pronoun.
Further, the 2 m. pl. imperat. qal שׁוּבוּ (repent, turn
ye) accords strangely with the following 3 pl. and its
subject, 'the sons of Israel'. Septuagint (Cod. B)
omits all reference to the sons of Israel, and makes
both verbs 2 m. pl. This is what all the Versions
have done, including RV, making 'sons of Israel'
a vocative, but AV and RVm are closer to the
Hebrew.

לַאֲשֶׁר. The prep. *lamedh* has no support in the
Versions, but T, V and S support the reading כַּאֲשֶׁר
('in as much as' or 'since', BDB 455*b*), which makes

good Hebrew. For the rest, read תַּעֲמִיקוּ and follow RV. סרה is a noun in the accusative meaning 'apostasy'.

Verse 7. ימאסון, 3 m. p. imf. qal of מאס I (reject) in pause with full ending, GK 47*m*; 'they shall reject each man his silver nothings'.

לכם ידיכם. Here again we have the curious anomaly of the previous verse of 2 m. pl. allied with 3 m. pl., but the verse makes sense without any change.

חטא. Most moderns omit as a gloss. LXX has apparently (ἄνομον) transferred the word to the end of the previous verse, where it might very well belong, and so form a couplet.

Verse 8. לא־איש. The negative לא is a deliberate denial that the sword is human. The ordinary negative אין would have been nothing more than a plain, ordinary statement.

לוֹ. This is the Western reading and the Eastern Qere, and so T and S. It is the 'ethical dative', throwing the emphasis back on the subject in order to express emphasis, WL 207 (ii), GK 119*s*, 135*i*. The Eastern Kethib is לא, and so LXX and V, influenced doubtless by the two negatives earlier in the verse.

חרב. According to GK 125*c*, the lack of determination in this noun is the Arabic 'indetermination for the sake of completeness', and it should therefore be translated 'an irresistible sword'. The absence of the article, frequent in poetry and exalted prose, makes it dangerous always to assume the occurrence of what is a genuine Hebrew, as well as Arabic, idiom.

בחוריו. Note the firm *pathach* which occurs in all plural forms of בָּחוּר, GK 84ᵃ*m*, 84ᵃ*g*.

לָמַס, 'for forced labour' (i.e. the *corvée*). The *qamets* is not due to the article (which would be לְמַם), but is the long vowel of the pretone, DG 51, WL 45, GK 102*f*.

Verse 9. 'And his rock (crag) because of terror shall he overpass (pass by), and his princes shall be terrified from the standard', i.e. they will all be so terrified that they will flee straight past their rallying-place of refuge. Neither AV nor RV are very satisfactory, and all the ancient Versions found difficulty. Most moderns radically reconstruct the text, and perhaps Kittel's suggestion is least unsatisfactory, וְסֹעֲרוּ מִמָּצֹור גִּבּוֹרִים, 'and the heroes shall be storm-driven from the strong-hold'. Then for מנם follow Cheyne, Procksch and others with מִמָּנוֹם, 'from refuge', since the Versions generally understand the latter part of the line to have something to do with 'flight'.

CHAPTER XXXII

Verse 1. לצדק. Prep. *lamedh* here denotes the principle according to which the act is done; cf. xlvi. 3, לאמת (faithfully), Jeremiah ix. 2, לאמונה (honestly), WL 207 (iii), GK 119*r*.

ולשׂרים, 'and as for princes', but it is better to treat the *lamedh* as the error of an early copyist, and to read, with Versions and moderns, וְשָׂרִים.

יָשֹׁרוּ, 3 m. p. imf. qal of שׂרר (rule), a denominative from שַׂר.

Verse 2. אישׁ. Either 'each one' (Gesenius, Ewald, Skinner) or better, 'a great man' (Cheyne). This is

66

the Arabic construction mentioned in the note on
xxxi. 8. The reference is to the Messianic Saviour,
no ordinary man, but one of exceptional virtues, the
King of verse 1.

מחבא, cstr. sing. of a substantive from the root חבא
(hide), found only here.

זרם. All assume the reading מִזֶּרֶם (from a rain-
storm). Box would transfer כָּבֵד from the following
line. It is not in V, and this line is short just as the
next one is long. Translate, in this case, 'and a covert
from a heavy rainstorm'. The text of LXX seems to
bear little resemblance to the Hebrew in this verse
and the next, so that it is hazardous to make any
reconstruction on the basis of it.

Verse 3. תשעינה, 3 f. p. imf. qal of שעה (behold), but
this makes no sense. The English Versions have
followed the ancient Versions, except for LXX, which
seems to have read the root שען (lean, support oneself),
and have read תִּשָּׁעֶינָה, 3 f. p. imf. qal of שעע I (be
smeared over, blinded), so Ewald and almost all
moderns; cf. xxix. 9. Gesenius-Buhl would read the
hophal, but this is not necessary, though suggested by
the hiphil in vi. 10. Sym. has ἀμαυρωθήσονται (be
dim), V has *caligabunt* (steam, be blind), whilst T has
the root סתם (stop, close up).

Verse 4. נמהרים, m. pl. ptc. niph. of מהר (hasten,
hurry). The 'hasty' of the margins of the English
Versions is accurate. The reference is to the ignorant
man who blurts out ill-considered opinions.

לדעת, prep. *lamedh* plus inf. cstr. qal of ידע (know),
with the first *qamets* in the pretone (DG 51, WL 45,
GK 102*f*), and the second in pause with *athnach* for
pathach; 'shall understand so as to know'.

67

עִלְּגִים, m. pl. of עִלֵּג (stammerer). The form denotes physical infirmity, GK 84ᵇd.

צָחוֹת, f. pl. of צַח (dazzling, clear), 'clear things'; cf. the 'plainly' of the English Versions. The first vowel is *qamets*, according to the majority of the best authorities, though Jacob ben Chaim has *pathach*. Most moderns omit the word as a gloss. LXX and S have 'peace'..

Verse 5. לֹא. A number of MSS. (ten Kennicott and two Ginsburg) prefix *vav*, assimilating to the Versions. Translate 'and no longer shall the vile person be called noble, and the knave shall not be said to be noble'. The last word is said to be either from the root ישׁע (with an original meaning 'to be spacious' and so 'to be free') or from a secondary form ישׁוע, in either case to mean 'free', and so 'independent', and ultimately 'noble' both in rank and (as here) in character. The Versions found it difficult to fix the precise sense of any of the four conduct-words, but the general sense is clear. Both verbs are in the niphal, the use being passive with the true subject introduced by the prep. *lamedh* and the remoter object in the accusative. DS 113 (Rem. 2), GK 121a.

Verse 6. יַעֲשֶׂה־. So S, but the other Versions presuppose יַחֲשֹׁב־ (shall devise), which some moderns follow, but there is no need so readily to assume that MT must be wrong, especially when one Version supports it.

חֹנֶף, 'profaneness', the noun being found only here. The line is short, and it may be that a word has dropped out, but the Versions give no help. Perhaps insert בְּעֶלְיוֹן (against the Most High) with Kittel, or וָרָע (and evil) with Procksch.

68

תּוֹעָה. The word means 'error', and in Rabbinic Hebrew 'heresy'.

לְהָרִיק . . . . Box translates 'in keeping the hungry unsatisfied', lit. 'to empty (hiph. inf. cstr.) the hungry appetite'.

מַשְׁקֶה. The best authorities make the final vowel *seghol*, in which case it is the absolute, and not the construct sing., and the translation is 'and he causeth the thirsty to lack drink', the intransitive verb becoming transitive in the hiphil, DS 105. If *tsere* be read, then the translation is: 'and the drink of the thirsty he causeth to fail'.

Verse 7. וְכֵלַי . . . . Rodwell, quoted by Cheyne, preserves the assonance with 'and as for a mean man, his means are evil'.

זִמּוֹת. The root is זמם (devise, plan). The noun is found 29 times, and always in a bad sense, except in Job xvii. 3. The fem. pl. is used for the classical neuter, DS 16, GK 122*q*.

יָעָץ, 3 m. s. pf. qal with *qamets* for *pathach* in pause with *zaqeph-qaton*.

עֲנָוִים. The Kethib is עֲנָוִים, m. pl. of עָנָו. The Qere is עֲנִיִּים, m. pl. of עָנִי. See note on xxix. 19.

וּבְדַבֵּר . . . . 'and when the poor speaketh right', i.e. with right on his side. This is the reading of V, but the other Versions presuppose וּבְדַבָּר אֶבְיוֹן בְּמִשְׁפָּט, 'and with a word the poor in judgement', and so Duhm and moderns generally.

Verse 9. נָשִׁים, pl. of אִשָּׁה (woman), DG 153, WL 185. The word is in the vocative. It is usual for the vocative to have the article, but not essential, DS 27, GK 126*f*.

שַׁאֲנַנּוֹת. The root is שׁאן (be at ease), and is always

69

found in Hebrew with the final radical doubled. In the case of this adjective the second *nun* is doubled with all suffixes. This is said to be in order to keep the previous vowel short (so GK 84[b]k), but it is more likely to be *dagesh forte firmativum* in order to strengthen the weak *nun* (GK 20k), the vowel then being necessarily short because of the rules of the Masoretes.

קמנה, 2 f. p. imperat. qal of קוּם (arise). Duhm and many moderns who are firm adherents to strict metrical rules would omit this word, but it is in all the Versions.

האזנה, 2 f. p. imperat. hiph. of אזן (give ear).

Verse 10. . . . ימים. Not, as in AV and RV, for a long time beyond a year, but 'in little more than a year'.

תרגזנה, 2 f. p. imp. qal of רגז (tremble, be excited, perturbed).

כלה, prophetic perfect, DS 61, DT 20, GK 106n.

אסף, 'ingathering', here probably the vintage itself, but it is also the name of the great pilgrimage feast of the vintage which in pre-exilic times marked the end of one year and the beginning of the next.

בלי is a negative, usually with an adjective or participle, and very rare with the finite verb. The root is בלה (wear out, waste away).

Verse 11. חרדו, 2 m. p. imperat. qal of חרד (tremble). The masc. is unusual in addressing feminine persons, but it is not otherwise unknown, GK 110k. All the verbs in this verse are strange, and are explained as aramaizing forms of 2 f. pl. It is probably best also to read חֲרָדָה or חֶרְדָּה, and so make it conform with the rest.

Verse 12. The verse is difficult, partly because it seems to have a line too many, and partly because of the strange m. pl. ptc. The translation of MT is 'lamenting upon the breasts, for the pleasant fields, for the fruitful vine'.

עַל־שָׁדַיִם, 'upon the breasts', and so all the Versions, this seeming to be demanded from the following word. On the other hand, the rest of the verse demands עַל־שָׂדִים, 'for the fields', a reading (though an unusual pl.) which has the additional merit of giving the same meaning to the preposition throughout the verse. Marti would omit 'upon the loins' from the previous verse, 'upon the breasts (for the fields)' from this verse, point סְפֹדָה ('lament', making another aramaizing imperative), and add it to the previous verse. This avoids the extra line, gets rid of the strange m. pl. ptc., and reduces the tautology (if 'fields' is right) in verse 12. This is as good a solution as most. An alternative, which we prefer, is to retain everything, and read 'Gird (sackcloth) upon the loins, lament for the fields, שָׂדִים; for the pleasant field, for the fruitful vine (verse 13), for the land of my people'. Tautology is no weakness in Hebrew verse. The RV 'smite' follows LXX, but has no other justification.

שְׂדֵי, cstr. sing. of שָׂדֶה (field) for the normal שָׂדֶה, which 21 Hebrew MSS. read here, LXX, V and some moderns. The alternative is to regard it as a parallel cstr. pl. to the normal שְׂדוֹת, GK 93*ll*, BDB 961*a*; cf. Ruth i. 6.

Verse 13. יַעֲלֶה. This is usually parsed as 3 f. s. impf. qal, '(which, i.e. the cultivated land) goes up in thorns, briers'. But it is better to regard it as the hiphil (cf. xl. 31, which is best taken as a hiphil, see the commentaries), and to translate: 'It shall grow (i.e. cause to come up) . . .'.

קוֹץ שָׁמִיר. Not 'briers and thorns', but 'thorn-briers', taking the second word as in apposition to the first, and denoting a particular kind of desert-thorn. The קוֹץ could grow anywhere, but the שָׁמִיר (found of 'thorns' only in Isaiah) belongs definitely to the waste lands, and is the 'thorn of the desert', Judges viii. 7, 16. See DS 40*f*, GK 131*b*.

כִּי. This seems to be one of the cases where כִּי is not a conjunction, but a particle with an intensive force, BDB 472 (section *e*). So V, but the other Versions presuppose וְעַל, which Kissane follows. Kittel and Procksch would delete.

קריה . . . is best taken as in loose apposition to the previous construct phrase, DS 37 (Rem. 3). According to GK 128*c*, the previous מָשׂוֹשׂ is an anomalous cstr. sing., but it is not necessary to assume this.

Verse 14. נֻטַּשׁ, 3 m. s. pf. pual of נטש (forsake), with *qamets* for *pathach* in pause with *zaqeph-qaton*. Similarly, the following verb has *qamets* in pause with *athnach*. Prophetic perfects.

עפל. The aristocratic part of the city near the royal palace. The 'darkness' of Vulgate and Douai is due to reading an *aleph* for an *ayin*, and the following 'obscurity' is doubtless a guess. So also is the 'watch tower' of the English Versions. בַּחַן is probably a particular part of the city, just as is Ophel.

בעד is very difficult and must be translated 'are to come to be on behalf of (i.e. take the place of) caves', but it is best to assume that it is a dittograph of the three letters which follow, so Graetz and moderns. Bickel and Marti suggest לְבָעֵר (it shall be for burning); cf. Isaiah v. 5, etc.

72

מְעָרוֹת, 'caves, dens', from the root ערר I, but Duhm
and Box prefer מַעֲרֶה (a bare spot), from the root ערה
(be naked, bare).

עַד־עוֹלָם. Many moderns omit on dogmatic grounds.

Verse 15. יערה, 3 m. s. impf. niph. of ערה (be naked,
bare), usually translated 'until there be poured' under
the influence of the Vulgate *effundatur*, and perhaps also
the use of the root in Isaiah liii. 12 and in Psalm
cxli. 8 as a simile for death, i.e. making naked the
nephesh to death. LXX and T have the simple 'come',
whilst Syriac reads יֵעֹר (3 m. s. impf. niph. of עוּר I),
'until there be roused', which may well be the original
intention of the writer. עַד is properly a preposition,
and needs the addition of אֲשֶׁר to make it into a conjunction, but it is used frequently as a conjunction,
followed, as here, by the finite verb. Note that the
rendering 'until the spirit be poured . . .' presupposes
the infrequent masc. gender for רוח.

וכרמל. The Qere inserts the article as is usual.

Verse 17. מעשה, cstr. sing. of מַעֲשֶׂה, usually 'work',
but here 'effect of working'; cf. עָוֹן, which means both
'iniquity' and 'punishment' as being the effect of
iniquity.

. . . ועבדת. Most moderns would read 'and the
result (effect of working) of justice shall be trust',
reading משפט for צדקה, partly to provide a true parallel,
and partly assuming a corruption of השׁקט. There is
no support for this in the Versions.

Verse 18. מבטחים. Some editions and the majority
of MSS. have *qamets* under *cheth*, but the best authorities
have *pathach*.

Verse 19. וברד. 'But it shall hail', as RV, the verb

73

being a denominative of בָּרָד (hail), though in this case the qal is unusual, since we would expect the piel. Read either וּבָרָד, 'and (there shall be) hail in the downfall (prep. *beth* plus inf. cstr. qal) of the forest', or וְיָרַד, 'and down shall come with a downfall the forest, and in lowliness (LXX Codd. A and B have "as in lowliness") shall the city be laid low'.

Verse 20. זֹרְעֵי, cstr. pl. of act. ptc. qal of זרע (sow) but with a prep. following anomalously as is sometimes found, DS 37, GK 130*a*.

Printed in Great Britain by
The Camelot Press Ltd., London and Southampton